Ingredients

A large dollop of fun
Several spoons of common sense
A portion of imagination
A dose of preparation
A pinch of your inner child
A sprinkling of order
A large cup of love

Method

Combine the preparation and order in a large bowl until smooth. Then, using little spoons, forks and fingers, whisk together the common sense, imagination and inner child until the mixture is colourful and full of enthusiasm. Mix the fun and love together in a separate bowl, then slowly fold into the colourful, enthusiastic batter. Pour the mixture into a beautiful, yet simple, mould and pop it in the oven. Refer to it regularly while your children are growing up, then hold onto it until you have grandchildren and refer to it again.

Hannah Bennett

The tickle fingers Toddler Cookbook

Hands-on fun in the kitchen for 1 to 4s

Annabel Woolmer

Vermilion
LONDON

To my Mum for teaching me, and to John and my girls, with love.

10 9 8 7 6

Vermilion, an imprint of Ebury Publishing,
20 Vauxhall Bridge Road,
London SW1V 2SA

Vermilion is part of the Penguin Random House group
of companies whose addresses can be found at global.
penguinrandomhouse.com

Text and photographs copyright © Annabel Woolmer 2016
Illustrations copyright © John Woolmer 2016
Poem page 1 copyright © Hannah Bennett 2016

Annabel Woolmer has asserted her right to be identified as
the author of this Work in accordance with the Copyright,
Designs and Patents Act 1988

Produced by Bookworx
Project editor: Jo Godfrey Wood
Project designer: Peggy Sadler

First published by Vermilion in 2016
www.penguin.co.uk

A CIP catalogue record for this book is available from the
British Library

ISBN 9781785040566

Printed and bound in Italy by L.E.G.O. S.p.A.

Penguin Random House is committed to a sustainable future
for our business, our readers and our planet. This book is
made from Forest Stewardship Council® certified paper.

Contents

All about Tickle Fingers

When my eldest was about 13 months old, we were living in a small, temporary flat with few toys and no transport. I was rapidly running out of entertainment ideas when I decided to attempt baking with her.

To encourage them to use their fingertips, I tell them to pretend they are tickling the butter into the flour. We call this process 'tickle fingers'.

We sat together on the kitchen floor and made a childhood favourite of mine, chocolate fork biscuits (see page 66). She prodded the mixture, squished it in her hands and, of course, licked the bowl. It kept her happy for about half an hour and then even happier once the biscuits were ready to eat. There was mess to clean up (mainly on her), but remarkably little. Result? Happy mum, happy baby! It got me thinking that I should do more cooking with her.

Over the coming months that's what I did, especially after her sister was born, as it gave us treasured one-on-one time together. She got increasingly involved and by age two, like it or not, I had a permanent 'helper' whenever I was in the kitchen. However, being short of time, with a young baby, I needed to get on with feeding the family, not just making fun cakes and biscuits.

I bought some children's cookbooks and looked online, hoping to find dishes my daughter could make to serve at family meals. What I found were either recipes for fun snacks and children's food or ones that she couldn't do at her age without a lot of help. Most of the latter were too long and included steps that she couldn't carry out safely, such as handling raw meat, using sharp knives/graters or stirring pans at a hob. The recipes advised that an adult should step in to do these bits, but I found that unworkable. She either got bored while waiting, or frustrated, shouting 'I do it, I do it'.

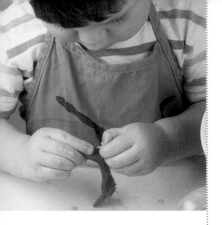

After buying children's cookbook number five, I gave up and decided to create my own recipes. I put together dishes that only involved cooking tasks she could do easily herself – sorting, mixing, squishing, bashing, pouring, covering, squeezing, tearing – and avoided tasks she couldn't. I kept the recipes short, limiting ingredients and steps. I was more relaxed because she was happily engaged doing fun tasks with minimal input from me. And the more independence and control over the cooking I gave her, the more enthusiastic and skilful she became. Then I realised she was developing a curiosity about food that I hadn't noticed before. Excited and proud about having cooked it 'all by herself', she was eating ingredients and dishes she had previously refused to taste. Even when she hadn't cooked the food herself, she was more interested in what I cooked and intrigued about new dishes rather than fearing and rejecting them.

The key to successfully cooking with very young children is to keep things simple.

I can't remember a time when I didn't know how to cook. It was just something that was always going on at home. I'm no expert cook and continue to learn every day, but my mum gave me the foundations to build on; something I will always be grateful for and want for my own children. Starting to cook with them aged 18 months might seem young and for that reason fool-hardy. It wasn't part of a grand plan; I fell into it. However, now that I've seen the benefits, it doesn't seem so crazy. It's odd that few of us question doing art, crafts and play dough with toddlers and yet the idea of cooking with them, using identical skills, is often still seen as daunting. This book aims to make cooking undaunting and approachable, particularly for those who don't feel confident in the kitchen themselves.

The key to successfully cooking with very young children is to keep things simple. Cooking with children can be stressful, but the stress largely comes from attempting over-ambitious recipes and not preparing enough beforehand. The simplicity of the recipes and layout in this book (e.g. Parent Prep) are intended to make things as straightforward and stress-free as

Why cook with tiny tots?

I believe cooking at a very young age has enhanced my children's lives in the following ways:

'Thanks for our food!'
A meal does not magically appear for them to accept or reject. Their direct involvement, or even just awareness of what goes into preparing a meal, gives them an interest in the outcome.

'Can I try that?'
I am convinced that cooking has increased their interest in food and therefore given them a willingness to try new things. And this has helped us to create a more enjoyable atmosphere around meal times.

'I can do it now!'
Watching my normally fidgety two-year-old carefully spoon flour into a bowl without spilling any has convinced me of the benefits for her focus and dexterity.

'I did it by myself!'
Children love the idea that they've made something themselves for us all to enjoy. We always make a big play of thanking whoever was the 'little chef', just like they have to thank mum or dad for their meal.

'Cooking is fun!'
It is always a struggle to find time to do fun things together. I know I am always promising them we'll get the paints out 'tomorrow', only to find it's the end of the week and I still haven't. Cooking with small kids does take longer, but by involving them, we are doing something fun and constructive that needed doing anyway.

possible, including the shopping. I've tried to stick to common, everyday ingredients that you can pick up in most local mini supermarkets. However, simplicity does not have to mean that the food is tasteless. As anyone with a brilliant home-cook for a mum, like me, will know, you can have both simplicity and yummy food at the same time.

When I have an uninterrupted day to myself, I love to try out new, complex dishes. But now that I'm a mum, those days are rare. Most of the time, I just need 'quick' and 'tasty' food that all the family will enjoy. And when I am involving the children in the cooking, this is even more the case. With that in mind, the recipes in this book are full of shortcuts and sometimes make compromises to keep things easy. They are not about producing the 'best of something you've ever tasted' to impress with at a dinner party. They are

about making it possible for young children to become a central part of everyday cooking for the whole family to enjoy.

Many researchers believe that our long-term eating habits are formed in the first few years, making it all the more important to get early experiences with food right. However, while we need to be mindful about balancing our children's diet and watching salt and sugar intake, I don't think this means we need to beat ourselves up if they refuse a specific vegetable or are partial to a small slice of cake.

I think the best thing we can do is try to ensure that our children are exposed to, and become familiar with, a wide variety of real (not processed) food, are open to trying new things, and feel positive and relaxed about food and eating. I don't like the idea of labelling food as 'good' or 'bad'. At this early stage in their lives, I want children to see all food as being interesting and fun. So, while this book aims to encourage them to eat more fruit and veg and choose healthier options, it is not about achieving the healthiest-possible diet or avoiding all sugary treats. I've tried to include a wide range of recipes for lots of different occasions, all designed to encourage children to explore and have fun with food.

My final note is a plea to grown-ups. The hardest thing about cooking with very young children is to let go, especially as far as mess is concerned. But you are the key to success here. If you are relaxed and give your children independence, they may yet surprise you with how much they can do by themselves. Trying to cook with a toddler underfoot used to be the worst part of my day. Now we do it together and it's my favourite.

Enjoy!

Trying to cook with a toddler underfoot used to be the worst part of my day. Now we do it together and it's my favourite.

All you need to know

Before you start your first cooking session with your toddler, there are a few handy things to know to make things easier and more fun. Take a few minutes to read the following pages to pick up some tips and info about how to get the most from this book.

Why toddlers should cook

Cooking with, rather than for, toddlers needs quite a bit of preparation, it takes longer, makes more mess and can be a bit stressful. So why would you want do to it?

Turn your toddler into a 'positive eater'

I don't know of a single toddler who hasn't gone through a phase of picky eating – even if it turns out to be a short-lived spell. Something seems to happen when babies turn into toddlers: stubbornness, independence, the need for control and curiosity all appear from nowhere. And with these also comes a need for familiarity and security. Full of contradictions, new emotions and hormones, this is a tricky time for little ones and it's not surprising that meal times can be affected. Cooking food together can help to harness this desire for control and turn meals into positive events. It provides an opportunity for natural curiosity to take over, making children more likely to taste things they might not otherwise try. As they explore and have fun with each ingredient, they are building positive associations with food, which can help form a lifelong, good relationship with it.

I weaned both my children using the baby-led method, which gives babies control over what and how much they eat, helping to create a relaxed, happy environment around food. I see allowing toddlers to have fun preparing their own food as a natural extension of this approach. I am always surprised at the variety of food my children will try if they have cooked it themselves. They wouldn't have necessarily touched it if I had just given it to them.

I am always surprised at the variety of food my children will try if they have cooked it themselves.

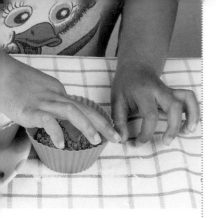

My favourite thing about cooking with toddlers is seeing their faces when they realise what they've achieved.

How cooking impacts early-years learning

Cooking can contribute to almost every area of how your toddler learns in the early years:

Communication and language

Even with the most basic cooking tasks, children are learning to listen and follow instructions. As you cook together talk about what they are doing and the ingredients being used (where they came from, texture, colour, taste and smell). When your children have finished cooking, go over what they did. When you are all sitting down to eat, get them to tell everyone what went into the dish (younger toddlers) or how they made it (older toddlers). They don't usually remember much and may need a lot of prompting, but they're getting used to the idea of re-telling an experience. If you can, cook with children one-on-one – it's less stressful, a great bonding time and it's easier to encourage communication and language.

Physical development

Cooking is non-stop motor-skill practice: controlling tools and picking up and handling food with fingers (the pincer movement). This all helps pencil control when they learn to write in future years. And learning experiences like washing hands, not touching hot things (the oven), exposure to a range of foods all help to develop children's knowledge of how to keep themselves safe and healthy.

Personal, social and emotional development

For me, personal development is the biggest reason to cook with toddlers. My favourite thing is seeing their faces when they realise what they've achieved. But this only happens if they feel 'in charge' of the kitchen, as though they've done it themselves. This is why I focus so much on making things achievable and allowing them as much independence as possible. They are the head-chef; you are the sous-chef!

Doing any activity one-on-one is quality time that promotes positive relationships. However, there is something special about preparing food together and then all sitting down and enjoying the results. It helps children learn respect for both food and its provider. By being involved in the process, children, even very young ones, are learning to appreciate the effort that goes into food preparation and to feel a central part of family meals.

Cooking provides lots of opportunities for emotional development. Children might be disappointed because something didn't work out how they wanted. They might find it frustrating to follow instructions, rather than do their own thing. Or they might feel out of their depth. Experiencing and handling these feelings in the security of the home environment can help children to learn how to deal with set-backs and challenges. So, if things don't go to plan, don't feel disheartened, treat it as a learning opportunity.

One, two, three: incorporating number skills

There are lots of ways you can incorporate basic number skills into cooking:

☺ Get your children to count out ingredients or spoonfuls. If they are not yet counting independently, count with them. Older children can add or take away and then re-count.

☺ Talk about what it means to split things in half (two pieces) or quarters (four pieces).

☺ Look out for basic shapes like circles, triangles and squares.

☺ Compare amounts or sizes – talk about whether something looks bigger or smaller, or fuller or emptier.

Understanding the world

As you cook, talk about:

☺ Which country does the dish come from?

☺ How does the food grow? On a tree? In the ground? In a hot place? From a seed?

☺ Where did the food come from? Talk about how it went from farm to shop to home. Help your children to grow their own herbs or a few vegetables to use in their cooking. Visit a pick-your-own farm and do a recipe together with what they've picked. Let them choose a fruit or vegetable in the supermarket and then cook with it.

All these things help to enthuse them about food and develop an understanding of the world around them.

Expressive art and design

Cooking is a constant exploration of colour, texture and form that also gives space for creativity and imagination. Talk with the children about how things change as they do different tasks: white to pink, lumpy to smooth. With older toddlers, ask them what they think will happen before they start.

Where the recipe allows, give children a chance to be creative. Let them choose which shaped cookie cutter to use. Lay out a selection of vegetables for them to taste and choose which to use in something like a pizza, tart or frittata. Let them decorate and present the dish how they like.

Effective learning

There are things that can make children better learners in all aspects of the cooking process:

☺ Playing and exploring helps them engage with an activity or experience.

☺ Active learning helps develop their concentration and staying-power.

☺ Creating and thinking critically helps with problem-solving and planning.

What age should we start?

The most common question I get asked is how old do they have to be? This is a difficult one – every child has their own character and develops differently. Here is some general guidance.

Don't be put off cooking with a child under two – it's such a great, tactile activity.

A child needs to be able to:

☺ Understand basic commands, like 'put those into there'.

☺ Be walking steadily, with reasonable hand control.

This stage could range from between one year and 18 months, or beyond. If you're not sure, give cooking a try. If things don't go well, you can always abandon the session and return to it when they're a bit older. Just don't expect too much, especially with very young ones. At the beginning you will probably have to step in a lot and you might have to try several times before they start to get the idea. I would say that between the ages of one and two you are preparing the ground. Between two and three is when, with practice, they are able to start cooking for themselves with minimal help.

Cooking with a one-year-old who has only recently mastered walking is a different prospect to cooking with a running, talking three-year-old. Things may not be entirely straightforward, but don't be put off cooking with a child under two – it's such a great, tactile activity, so your child will be benefitting from the experience, even if the end result is less than perfect.

Cooking with teeny tinies

Things to think about when your children are very small:

- **Focus on having fun with just a few ingredients,** rather than worrying about finishing the recipe. You can always finish it off for them if they lose interest.

- **Think about where they are going to cook.** Sitting them on a mat on the floor or in a highchair works well if they are a little unsteady on their feet.

- **Assume they will shove everything into their mouth.** Be extra careful with the ingredients and equipment you give them. For example, babies and toddlers shouldn't eat raw egg because of the danger of ingesting salmonella bacteria. Likewise fingers covered in raw meat, especially poultry, could cause dangerous food poisoning. While you might be able to explain this to a three- or four-year-old, in my experience you will struggle to stop a one-year-old from licking without confusing and upsetting them. If cooking with a very young toddler, or one who is determined to lick, cut down on stress by avoiding using egg and raw meat.

All the Easy Peasy-level recipes in this book are fine to lick while cooking and have fewer ingredients and steps. In other words, they are designed for very young toddlers or those starting to cook for the first time.

What do you need?

Very little. There is no need to buy lots of special children's kitchen equipment. They can use most of what you have already. However, here are some suggestions to make things easier and safer.

Small, low table

Use any table that is the right height for them to stand up at easily. You can also use the base of a chair, but you might find that lack of space is annoying. I don't recommend letting your toddler stand on a stool or chair at the worktop. Firstly, you don't want to spend the whole time worrying about them falling. And secondly, if your worktop is like mine, there are lots of things for them to fiddle with. At their own table you pass them what they need when they need it, avoiding distraction and keeping mess contained.

Apron

This keeps toddler clothes *slightly* cleaner, but the main point is the excitement they get from having and wearing their own.

Measuring cups and spoons

Most toddler attention spans mean that it is a good idea to weigh out ingredients before they start cooking. However, at some point you will probably want them to do a bit of measuring themselves. I find the best way is to use American-style cups and spoons so that they don't need to know how to read scales. All they have to do is fill the right cup or spoon, the right number of times. The sets of cups and spoons that come in different colours are great because you can explain measurements to them in terms of one

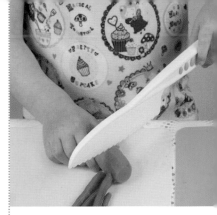

'yellow' cup, two 'blue' cups, etc. There is more information on this and a conversion table at the back of the book (see page 116).

Plastic or stainless-steel mixing bowls

Your choice of bowl will depend on your child's temperament. My older child was so careful that I was relaxed about using Pyrex mixing bowls without fear of them getting broken. When I tried cooking with my younger child, I quickly decided that there was a strong probability that the bowl would end up on the floor in a fit of enthusiasm, so I bought plastic.

Child-safe knives

A table knife is sufficient for all the recipes in this book. However, if you have an older toddler who wants to get more involved in food preparation, then you can buy serrated, child-safe knives that cut more easily.

Flour dredger

This is fun for sprinkling flour on a surface or rolling pin to stop sticking.

Silicone cupcake cases

Sticky mixtures tend to stick to paper cases, making them more fiddly for children to use. The silicone ones are easier, are reusable and can be bought in fun colours.

Non-stick baking mat

You can get these in different bright colours. They provide a hygienic surface to prepare food on, and when baking are easier to use than greaseproof paper.

Handled grater

This is only worth having for an older toddler who can wind the handle. You can also buy handled peelers/choppers for apples and potatoes, and others for finely chopping herbs.

How to make it fun

Cooking together is only fun when you are relaxed and they are happily engaged in what they are doing. Here are a few things you can do to help minimise the stress and keep your little chef happy.

Choose your recipe carefully

This book has lots of recipe ideas but you can also adapt recipes from adult books. Keep the following principles in mind:

☺ **The shorter the better.** Six ingredients and about five or six method steps is the most you can expect from the average toddler.

☺ **Avoid cooking on the hob.** As toddlers cannot cook on the hob safely, they have to watch you and wait. And, as with most things with toddlers, keeping up the momentum is key. The ideal recipe involves a few steps to assemble the ingredients and then into the oven or fridge.

☺ **In the early days, try to avoid ingredients you don't want your toddler to eat:** raw egg, raw meats, etc. It might take them time to learn not to stuff everything into their mouths. If it's something that could cause them harm, then the session becomes stressful rather than fun.

☺ **Don't choose a recipe by the pretty pictures alone.** The pictures of the food in this book are fairly ordinary. This is intentional. My pet peeve with children's cookbooks is the use of pictures of decorated food designed to attract children, but which they haven't a hope of recreating themselves. My daughter picks recipes because she likes the look of 'the little bees' or 'pink flowers' and is then disappointed when the end result doesn't look anything like the picture.

Let them choose

When possible, give them choices. For example, they can choose what pizza toppings to use, which fruit to put in the pudding, what shape to cut the biscuits. This is great for their creativity, but also increases their feeling of ownership and therefore enthusiasm.

Lay everything out before you start

This seems obvious, but I still find myself rummaging around to find a key ingredient while the children get bored and start mucking about with everything I've already got out: chaos and stress ensue and the momentum is gone! All the recipes have a Parent Prep section to help you set up more easily. It is also a good idea to fill a sink or bowl with soapy water and keep a towel handy so you can clean hands when necessary without having to break away from cooking. Or use wipes.

Get the children to do as much as possible

This ties in with choosing the right recipes – ones where the children can be involved throughout. Having said that, you will almost certainly need to step in to finish a task and perhaps move the recipe on to the next stage. For example, a toddler's idea of mixing is usually to prod it a few times. Encourage them to do more, show them what to do, encourage again and then help them to move on.

Avoid noisy kitchen gadgets

There are quicker and more effective ways to do many of the recipes in this book by using electric whisks and food processors and, in the right context, using an electric gadget can be fun for a child. However, I try to avoid them, firstly because it makes the recipes much more hands-on and secondly because many very young children don't like, or are even scared of, the noise these gadgets make.

Show them what to do, encourage again, and then help them to move on.

Timing, timing, timing

Picking the right time to cook with a young child is important. I have a tendency to decide just before lunch that we'll make something nice for pudding. Consequently we are in a rush, they are hungry, and it all goes wrong. Make sure you have minimal distractions and try to avoid cooking with children when they are hungry. They are going to struggle to concentrate if all they want to do is eat everything.

Talk to them

Find as many ways as you can to describe what the children have to do, the sillier the better. For example, mixing with a spoon could be 'a helicopter' or 'burying treasure under sand (flour)'. Sing a song which goes with the action, such as 'round and round the garden' for mixing. Use this opportunity to talk to them about the food: where it came from, its colour, its texture, its taste. It will all help them to understand what they are doing and to stay engaged.

Think about schemas

Schemas are ways in which toddlers play. The idea is that, if you can identify how they like to play, you can tailor the way you present learning activities, including cooking, to help them get the most from them. My eldest was a 'transporter'. She was always carrying something and used to push her baby pushchair up and down for hours. I used to do recipes with her that involved lots of moving of ingredients from one bowl to another. My youngest is an 'enveloper'. She likes to be hidden under things and covers the whole paper (and often her hands!) when painting or colouring – she enjoys cooking anything that means getting her hands into the mixture or wrapping or covering things up. She doesn't particularly like mixing. However, give a child who's a 'rotator' a mixing spoon and they will get stuck straight in.

Schemas won't always be obvious. Some toddlers have an obvious tendency towards a certain schema; others tend towards several and/or towards

If you can identify how they like to play, you can tailor the way you present learning activities, including cooking,

different ones at different stages. It's not something to get hung up on, but if you recognise a schema in your child, then it can be useful to think about which recipes or tasks they will engage with most. The chart (see page 29) is a brief overview of the main schemas and ideas for applying them to cooking. Every recipe also identifies which schemas it is particularly appropriate for and lists the main cooking tasks and skills.

Don't go for perfection

To me, the most important thing about cooking with a young child is that you have fun and end up with something tasty to enjoy together at the end. Don't worry about doing every stage perfectly or making the final result look dinner-party worthy. The recipes in this book are intentionally robust and forgiving. They allow for a bit of dropped flour here, or lump of butter there.

Stay calm

This is easier said than done when food is going everywhere, your toddler is trying to eat flour and the phone rings. But the most important thing is that it is fun for you both. If it isn't, stop and try again another time.

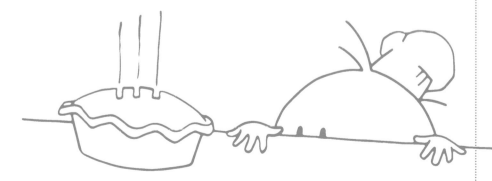

The schemas

Here is a brief overview of the main schemas and ideas for applying them to cooking. If you do identify one in your child, each recipe tells you which schema/s it is particularly appropriate for.

Schemas	What you might see in your child's play	Cooking tasks your child might like
Transporting	Pushing things around, carrying things	Spooning ingredients from place to place; counting out and measuring ingredients; chopping, tearing or snipping ingredients then putting them in a bowl; decorating dishes
Trajectory	Throwing, kicking, climbing, pouring	Pouring, spooning, sprinkling or squeezing ingredients, especially from a height; patting, pricking, bashing, chopping, shaking, tearing or breaking
Connecting	Jigsaws, building blocks, sequencing or laying things out	Constructing or layering; counting out ingredients; snipping, tearing or chopping then putting the dish together; decorating dishes
Transforming	Adding things to change them, for example water to sand, mixing paints	Mashing, mushing, crushing, bashing, rubbing, squishing, tearing, tickling or mixing ingredients to change texture or colour; folding or sculpting to change shape
Enveloping	Hiding, wrapping, layering, covering things or selves	Anything like rubbing, patting, crushing, squishing, tickling or mushing that involves getting hands into the mixture; burying, covering, wrapping up or layering ingredients; painting, spreading or coating
Containing	Filling and emptying things; climbing into boxes	Stuffing or spooning ingredients into things; measuring; wrapping things up
Rotating	Interest in things that go round: wheels, roundabouts	Mixing, whisking, rolling, twisting

Cooking tips

There are lots of different ways to make cooking techniques easier and more approachable for young children. You will come up with your own, but here are a few of the ones I use.

☺ **Softening butter: what to do if you forget to take it out of the fridge, or don't have time to let it go soft naturally**

Some of the recipes need softened butter. You need the butter to be soft enough for a young child to combine easily with another ingredient (think soft enough to squish easily with a finger). However, it is important to soften butter gently. Don't just whack it in the microwave or on the hob. This will change the properties of the butter and might cause the recipe to fail. If you have a microwave, heat the butter at 10–20% of its maximum power for 20 seconds at a time. Every 20 seconds, turn the butter so it softens evenly. You will probably have to do this between four and six times, depending on how hard the butter is.

☺ **Spooning sticky ingredients from one place to another**

The best way to do this is with two spoons, preferably metal ones. Ask your child to hold a spoon in each hand. Get them to scoop with one and scrape off the mixture with the other. If they struggle with this then you could do one spoon and they could do the other. I find it useful and fun to get them to name the spoons: for example, 'Topsy and Tim', 'Ben and Holly' or 'Peppa and George'. That way I can more easily explain what they are supposed to be doing with each spoon: for example, 'scoop up the mixture with Topsy' and 'scrape the mixture with Tim'.

☺ **Breaking eggs without getting shell in the mixture**

You need to get the children to pull the egg apart rather than crush it in their hands. To encourage this, I usually say a silly rhyme: 'Knock, knock on the door and open'. While singing this I get them to knock the egg on the rim of the bowl and then pull the two halves of the egg apart.

☺ **Combining butter and sugar**

The key to this with very young children is to have the butter as soft as possible, otherwise they will not be strong enough to combine it properly. Get them to squash the butter with the back of a wooden spoon and then stir. Keep doing this 'squash and stir' action. You might have to finish the process off, especially if the butter is a little too hard. Recipes often call for butter and sugar to be mixed until 'soft and fluffy', but the recipes in this book are robust enough that you don't need to worry about this; just get them combined.

☺ **Turning flour and butter into crumbs for pastry or crumble**

You want the children to rub the flour into the butter with their fingertips rather than squishing it together with their hands. If they squish, they could end up with a lump of dough rather than crumbs. To encourage them to use their fingertips, I tell them to pretend they are tickling the butter into the flour. We call this process 'tickle fingers'.

☺ **Cutting**

I strongly recommend that you never use a sharp knife, even if you are cutting with your children. I used to use one occasionally and hold the knife with them. Then one day in a moment of absentmindedness I put the knife down within reach of my two-year-old, who made a grab for it. Luckily she didn't hurt herself but I learnt my lesson. Now I do any cutting that needs a sharp knife and put it away before I get my children into the kitchen to cook. However, cutting is a useful skill for your children to learn. The recipes in this

book allow children to practise cutting soft foods with a table knife or a child-safe knife. Get them to tuck their thumb in when they hold the food. I tell my children to 'hide' their thumb in their hand. With the knife in the other hand, get them to do a sawing action forwards and backwards while pushing down on the food. This task needs close supervision and you will probably still need to hold the knife and food with your children long after they have mastered most of the other cooking skills.

☺ Bringing dough together
The aim is to get the children to put their hands in and squish. The heat of their hands will help to combine the mixture. Get them to take as big a handful as possible and squish and squeeze until it comes together.

☺ Rolling things out
Make sure they have prepared the area and the rolling pin with a good sprinkling of flour to prevent sticking. If you have a flour dredger then your children can have fun making it 'snow' everywhere.

The biggest mistake children make is to grip the rolling pin so that their fingers are in the way when they roll. Encourage them to spread their fingers, making 'stars' or a 'butterfly'. Adult rolling pins are better than children's ones because they have room to spread their hands out, and the weight helps them to compress the dough as they roll. Don't be surprised if your children struggle with rolling out. It is actually hard for young children to manage as it takes coordination and strength.

☺ Pinching
If your children need to pick up a pinch of flour to sprinkle it, get them to make a 'duck' or a 'parrot' with their hand, putting fingers and thumb together in a 'quack' or 'squawk'. Then get them to do the same action to pick up the flour. Then get them to rub their thumb over their fingers to sprinkle.

Ingredient tips

Toddlers are impatient. If they want to cook, they want to do it now! Keep key ingredients (see list below left) in stock ready for an impromptu session. And here are some more ingredient tricks to help you adapt your favourite dishes.

KEY INGREDIENTS

+ plain flour
+ self-raising flour
+ bicarbonate of soda
+ cocoa powder
+ sugar
+ eggs
+ chocolate chips
+ raisins
+ oats
+ vanilla extract
+ vegetable oil
+ Greek-style or natural yoghurt
+ butter

Onions Stews and curries often start with cooking chopped onions on the hob. One alternative is a spoonful of black onion (nigella) seeds. These give the flavour of onion without sharp knives and frying. Or, if the dish is tomato-based, then use a ready-made tomato pasta sauce because this will already have the cooked onion/garlic base. For a fresher onion taste, use spring onions, which the children can cut up using child-safe scissors.

Ready-made puff pastry The ultimate, easy-to-use, versatile toddler-chef ingredient. Buy ready-rolled if children are too young to handle a rolling pin. Put fruit on top for a sweet tart or pizza toppings for a savoury one. Use as a lid to top any filling you like to make a sweet or savoury pie.

Ready-made shortcrust (pie) pastry Making shortcrust pastry with a small child is good fun and do-able, but ready-rolled shortcrust is useful for speeding things up. Once you've got the base for a tart or quiche, there are lots of fillings that are easy for a small child to prepare and put in. Shortcrust is also fun to use to wrap ingredients up to make free-form pies.

Yoghurt This works as a binding agent so is a useful substitute for eggs. Use Greek-style or natural yoghurt, or a flavoured one to inject different flavours and/or more sweetness.

Vegetables Some vegetables are easy for small children to prepare and some are almost impossible without using a sharp knife or cooking first. Mushrooms, peppers, green beans, cabbage and broccoli can all be torn. Tomatoes, courgettes and aubergines can be chopped fairly easily using a table knife or child-safe knife. Sweetcorn (off the cob), peas and spinach can be used as they are. However carrots, potatoes and other root vegetables will need cooking first before they can be chopped safely.

Salt I don't like young children handling salt because it's hard for them to get the right amount into the dish and it's also not great if they decide to stuff it directly into their mouths. Using ingredients like bacon, a tinned soup, ready-made pasta sauce or cheddar cheese helps to provide flavour without the need for additional seasoning. But don't assume this means the dishes are salt-free; you're usually just adding salt in a different way. If the recipe does need a little salt, I add it to another dry ingredient when I am laying everything out so they don't have to handle it.

Sugar You can often reduce sugar in recipes, especially cakes and biscuits. And the more used children are to eating things with less sugar, the less of a sweet tooth they will have long-term. If you want to substitute refined sugar with honey, or similar, don't assume it's better for them – there is no consensus about this. I usually try to reduce sugar as much as possible, or leave it out.

Herbs These are a great way to add flavour to a simple dish and are easy for children to handle. They can tear herbs like basil and mint, which have larger leaves or use child-safe scissors to cut up parsley and chives. With young toddlers, chop the herbs beforehand for them to pinch and sprinkle on – a great pincer-movement practice for future writing skills. Most herbs are quick germinators, so fun for children to try growing themselves.

Trouble-shooting

As with any activity with young children, things aren't always straightforward. Here are some of the most common difficulties I've come across, with ideas on how to tackle them.

'When I try to cook with my daughter, she just wants to eat all the time. And when I won't let her because it's raw batter, she just gets upset.'
I think this is the number-one problem when cooking with very young children. You want them to be interested in the ingredients. You want them to be trying everything they can. But you don't want them sticking their hands in and eating things like raw egg. They don't understand when it's okay to eat and when it's not, so they get confused and upset.

Find a time to cook when the children are not hungry, such as just after snack time. Explain clearly that they can try things when you say it is okay. If you're cooking with something you don't want them to eat, like cake batter with raw egg, put out a bowl of something they can eat, like raisins. If they try to eat the batter, direct them to the bowl and say they can try that. Let them try as many of the ingredients as possible. But when you do, make a big thing of saying 'you can try this' so they learn it is okay when you give things to them, but not okay just to take stuff.

To try to avoid this problem, the Easy Peasy-level recipes only contain ingredients that won't matter if your children eat while they are cooking.

'**My son loves cooking. He wants to do it all the time. Sometimes I just need to get on with doing dinner, but he gets upset if I don't let him help.**'
You don't want to dampen his enthusiasm, but there will be plenty of times when you are doing things he can't help with. Try to find little things he can do to help, even if it's just putting cutlery on the table. I sometimes cut up the vegetables and then just get my daughter to put them into the pans (before they go on the heat!).

You could also try setting up a pretend kitchen. This doesn't have to be an expensive, shop-bought one: a cardboard box for an oven and some spare pots and pans and utensils will be fine. They can then be 'pretend' cooking alongside you while you get on with the real thing.

'**My son doesn't like getting his hands messy.**'
Some children do not like messy play. However, cooking could be a way for him to gain confidence with it. Choose recipes which don't involve sticking hands in, or do this bit for him (look out for the 'sticky fingers' alerts in the recipes). Get him to use spoons to move ingredients around. Don't push it. If your child's fear is extreme, get expert advice.

'**I really want to cook with my children, but I can't stand the mess.**'
Young children are going to make a mess, but I always think it's amazing how little they actually do make. If you invest in a small, low table and keep all the cooking your child does on that, any mess will be contained in one place. Nothing a quick wipe and sweep won't fix. You could even place a mat or plastic sheet under the table to catch any spills.

If you're still worried, once you've done the parent-preparation stage (Parent Prep), none of the recipes in this book requires you to actually be in a kitchen. You could lay out everything somewhere you don't mind getting messy, even outside.

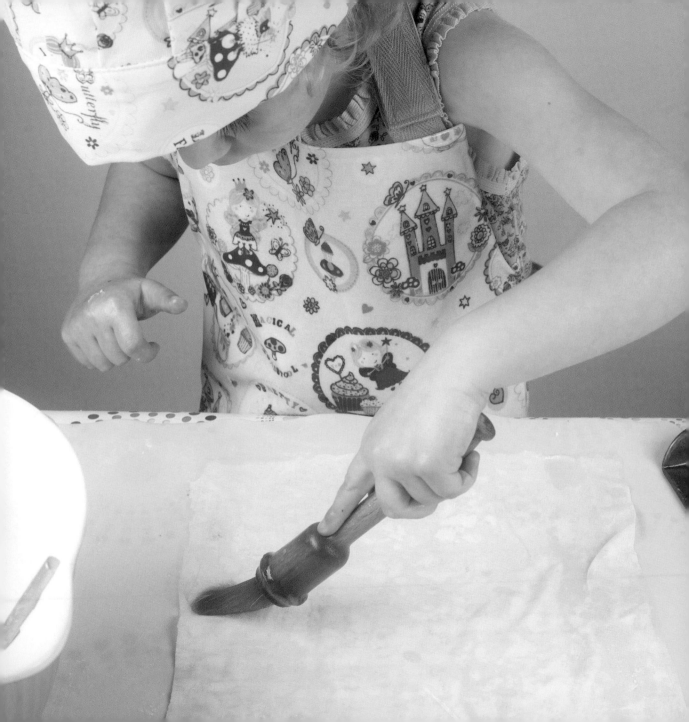

'I find it difficult not to step in and do it for her.'

Whether you're a good cook yourself and know how things 'should be done' or an inexperienced cook who is worried about getting it right, it's hard not to jump in when you see small children doing something imperfectly or slowly. Before intervening, ask yourself 'does this really matter?' If it's a case of something looking a bit wonky, having a small spill or taking five times as long to complete, it probably won't matter. Stand back and keep thinking about the satisfaction and confidence the children are getting from doing it themselves. That said, there will be times when they do need help. Just wait until they ask for it.

'I would love to do more cooking with my daughter, but every time we try she mucks around and I end up getting stressed with her.'

Cooking with a child who struggles with focus or following instructions is not easy. Choose the extra-short recipes. Don't cook at a worktop where there may be other things for her to investigate and get distracted by. Cook at her own child-height table and only give her what she needs as and when she needs it. If all she wants to do is play with the ingredients, don't worry too much. She may not be bothered about the end result; the fun for her might be all in the doing. So don't give her too many, or expensive, ingredients and just let her play. If you really want something edible at the end of the session, you can always try to cobble something together once she's lost interest.

Stand back and keep thinking about the satisfaction and confidence the children are getting from doing it themselves.

How to use this book

I have arranged this book to make it easy to find recipes to suit the occasion, your child, allergies, time available and the ingredients. Take a quick look through the features – and some other important notes – before you start.

The recipes are divided into four main sections:

☺ **Breakfast fun** Keep your children entertained first thing in the morning by letting them make breakfast for the rest of the family. Alternatively you can make many of the recipes the day before, ready for a quick breakfast the next day.

☺ **Snack time** Savoury and treat (biscuits and cakes) snacks presented in small batches for little hands and short attention spans.

☺ **Lunch for us** Light dishes for your children to prepare for lunch. Recipes serve two to three (one adult and two children or two adults and one small child).

☺ **Family supper** Main meals and puddings your children can make for the whole family to enjoy together. Recipes serve three to four (two adults and two children).

Preparation is a must for maintaining momentum and, therefore, your children's interest. So each recipe has a Parent Prep section for you to do first before involving your little chef. This includes equipment to lay out and any cooking preparation that would be difficult or unsafe for young children to do. This means that once the children start cooking, they are involved in every step until the dish goes into the oven, fridge or onto the table.

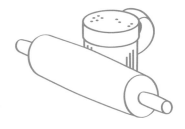

What are the levels of difficulty?

Every recipe has a level of difficulty denoted by a coloured tab at the top of the page.

 **EASY PEASY**    **BUDDING COOK**    **CONFIDENT CHEF**

Easy Peasy   For those just starting out, or the very young

Budding Cook   For those with a bit of experience

Confident Chef   For those who are ready for more of a challenge

Measurements are in metric and where appropriate, in American-style cups and spoons, so the children can do some of their own measuring. There is more on measuring in cups and a conversion table in the back of the book (see page 116). All tablespoon (tbsp) and teaspoon (tsp) measurements are level, unless it says otherwise.

Timings are shown by two clocks: Activity and Oven/Chill. The Activity timing is an estimate of how long it will take your children to do their bit. Bear in mind that this will vary a lot, depending on the age and speed of your children. Something a three-year-old might do in a minute could take an 18-month-old five minutes or more. But the timings should give you an idea and help you find recipes to suit your children's concentration spans.

 **Sticky fingers alerts** indicate a step that involves getting particularly sticky hands. Lots of children love getting food all over their hands, but some don't like the sensation. If your children fall into the latter category, you might want to avoid the recipe altogether or do these bits for them.

Main skills and tasks tells you the sorts of things the children will be doing. If they particularly enjoy certain cooking tasks, it will help you find other recipes they might like to try too.

Schemas are something that, if you identify them in your children, can help you pick recipes they will particularly enjoy or tailor how you approach cooking with them. There is more information on this on page 26.

Oven temperatures are for a standard oven. If you are using a fan oven, you need to lower the temperature – usually by about 20 degrees – but check your oven's instructions.

Allergies to things like milk-protein and egg are more prevalent in very young children, making allergy information all the more important. Each recipe contains ideas for allergy substitutions and there is an allergy chart at the back of the book (see pages 118–120) to help you find appropriate recipes and avoid inappropriate ones.

Food waste is something I hate, for environmental and cost reasons. I have intentionally duplicated ingredients in multiple recipes so that if you have something left over you can use it up on another day in another recipe. I have also included several recipes to use up things like leftover meat and vegetables. There is a list at the back of the book (see pages 121–123) to help you find what you can cook, depending on what you have available or need to use up.

Breakfast fun

Keep an early riser entertained making breakfast before the rest of the family wakes up. Or put them in charge of making a special weekend breakfast for everyone. These recipes also work as snacks, light meals or puddings.

Blueberry yoghurt muffins

These aren't the fluffiest of muffins, but lack of eggs and the throw-everything-into-a-bowl-and-mix concept is perfect for young toddlers to manage.

MAKES

4

 ACTIVITY **15**

 OVEN **20**

Your child's schemas
(see pages 26–29)
- Rotating
- Containing

Main tasks & skills
- Mixing
- Spooning
- Counting

Allergy information

Egg	Not applicable
Dairy	Use dairy-free yoghurt
Gluten	Use gluten-free flour and ½ a beaten egg
Nut	Check labels for potential contamination

WHAT YOU NEED

- 3 tbsp vegetable oil
- 4 tbsp Greek-style or blueberry yoghurt
- ½ tbsp honey
- 20 g (¼ cup) blueberries
- 65 g (½ cup) self-raising flour
- ⅛ tsp bicarbonate of soda

PARENT PREP

- Preheat oven to 180°C/350°F/Gas 4
- Lay out: ingredients, bowl, mixing spoon, 2 tablespoons, 4 cupcake cases and a cupcake tray

SERVING SUGGESTIONS

Great grab-and-go breakfast or serve warm with cream for pudding

ALL TOGETHER NOW!

❶ Put the oil, yoghurt, honey and blueberries into the bowl and mix.

❷ Add the flour and bicarbonate of soda. Mix until combined.

❸ Count out 4 cases into the tray.

❹ Use 2 spoons to scrape the mixture into the cases until each is two-thirds full.

AND FINALLY…

Bake in the oven for 20 minutes until they feel springy on top.

Overnight oats

Easiest made the day before for a grab-from-the-fridge breakfast the next morning. This is a good recipe for early measuring practice.

WHAT YOU NEED
+ 4 tbsp oats
+ 4 tbsp Greek-style or natural yoghurt
+ 4 tbsp blueberries, frozen or fresh
+ ½ tbsp runny honey

PARENT PREP
+ Lay out: ingredients, mixing bowl, mixing spoon, 2 tablespoons and 2 small jars with lids

SERVING SUGGESTIONS
Also makes a great snack or pudding

ALL TOGETHER NOW!

❶ Put the oats, yoghurt, blueberries and the honey into the bowl.

❷ Mix thoroughly.

❸ Spoon and scrape half the quantity into one jar and half into the other.

❹ Put on the lids.

AND FINALLY...

Put into the fridge for a minimum of 1 hour.

MAKES
2

ACTIVITY 10   CHILL 60

Your child's schemas
(see pages 26–29)
• Transforming   • Containing
• Rotating

Main tasks & skills
• Measuring   • Spooning
• Mixing

Allergy information

Egg	Not applicable
Dairy	Use dairy-free yoghurt
Gluten	Oats usually okay, but check label for potential contamination
Nut	Check labels for potential contamination

Baked eggs Benedict

This is a fun way for young children to make a special breakfast or light meal for the family. Hollandaise can be sharp for little taste buds so I often use mayonnaise.

SERVES
2–4

ACTIVITY
10

OVEN
15

Your child's schemas
(see pages 26–29)
- Transporting
- Enveloping
- Connecting

Main tasks & skills
- Painting
- Layering
- Tearing

Allergy information

Egg	Avoid
Dairy	Check muffin label
Gluten	Check muffins label
Nut	Check labels for potential contamination

WHAT YOU NEED
- 1 tbsp olive oil
- 2 English muffins
- 4 eggs
- 4 slices ham
- 4 tbsp hollandaise (optional)

PARENT PREP
- Preheat oven to 190°C/375°F/Gas 5
- Lay out: ingredients, oven-proof dish and pastry brush

ALL TOGETHER NOW!

❶ Use a pastry brush to brush oil all over the inside of the dish.

❷ Tear the ham into pieces and put all over the bottom of the dish.

❸ Tear the muffins into bite-sized pieces and put on top of the ham.

❹ Break the eggs onto the muffins, trying not to break the yolks.

AND FINALLY...

Bake in the oven for 12–15 minutes until the egg whites are white and cooked. Serve with a dollop of hollandaise (optional).

Baked pancake

This recipe involves lots of what my youngest calls 'crazy whisking'. Baked pancake has all the flavour of pancake but without the frying and tossing in a hot pan.

WHAT YOU NEED
- 50 g (⅓ cup) plain flour
- ⅛ tsp salt
- 90 ml milk
- 2 eggs
- 1 tsp butter
- Pancake topping of your choice

PARENT PREP
- Preheat oven to 200ºC/390ºF/Gas 6
- Lay out: ingredients, 20-cm-square cake tin (or ovenproof dish), mixing bowl and hand whisk

ALL TOGETHER NOW!

❶ Put the flour and salt into the bowl.

❷ Break the eggs into the bowl.

❸ Pour in half the milk. Whisk until combined.

❹ Add the rest of the milk and whisk again until bubbly.

❺ ✋ Rub the butter all over the cake tin.

❻ Pour the batter into the tin.

AND FINALLY...

Bake in the oven for 15 minutes until golden and fluffy. Take out of the hot tin and put onto a plate. Then get the children to decorate with their choice of toppings.

SERVES
2–4

ACTIVITY
15

OVEN
15

Your child's schemas
(see pages 26–29)
- Transforming
- Rotating
- Trajectory
- Enveloping

Main tasks & skills
- Whisking
- Pouring
- Rubbing
- Decorating

Allergy information

Egg	Avoid
Dairy	Use dairy-free milk
Gluten	Use gluten-free flour
Nut	Check labels for potential contamination

Bacon & egg soda bread

Soda bread is a nice and easy bread to make with toddlers because it involves very little kneading and no proving.

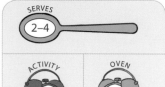

SERVES

2–4

ACTIVITY **20**

OVEN **40**

Your child's schemas
(see pages 26–29)
- Transforming
- Enveloping
- Rotating

Main tasks & skills
- Tearing
- Squishing
- Mixing
- Painting

Allergy information

Egg	Use milk to brush top
Dairy	Use dairy-free milk and yoghurt
Gluten	Use gluten-free flour
Nut	Check labels for potential contamination

WHAT YOU NEED
- 125 g (1 cup) plain flour
- 80 g (⅓ cup) Greek-style or natural yoghurt
- 1 tbsp milk
- ¼ tsp bicarbonate of soda
- 2 slices streaky bacon
- 1 egg

PARENT PREP
- Fry bacon and leave to cool
- Preheat oven to 150ºC/300ºF/Gas 2
- Lay out: ingredients, mixing bowl, mixing spoon, small bowl, fork, table knife, pastry brush and baking tray

VARIATION
For basic soda bread, swap bacon for ⅛ tsp salt and brush with milk not egg

ALL TOGETHER NOW!

❶ Tear the bacon into pieces and put it in the bowl.

❷ Add the flour, yoghurt, milk and bicarbonate of soda to the bowl and mix together.

❸ Squish and squash the dough with hands until it is combined.

❹ Put the ball of dough on the tray and use a table knife to cut a cross about 2 cm deep in the top.

❺ Break the egg into the small bowl and whisk with a fork until it is yellow.

❻ Use a pastry brush to paint the egg all over the dough.

AND FINALLY…

Bake for 40 minutes until the bottom sounds hollow when you tap it.

Kedgeree

This yummy old-school dish is traditionally eaten at breakfast. But if you don't fancy fish that early in the day, it makes a great lunch or light supper dish.

WHAT YOU NEED

- 100 g (½ cup) long-grain rice
- 120 ml (½ cup) single cream
- 1 tsp curry powder
- 150 g (1 cup) frozen peas
- 150 g (1¼ cups) boneless smoked mackerel
- 2 eggs
- Small handful parsley (optional)

PARENT PREP

- Cook rice or use 250 g (2 cups) leftover cooked rice
- Hard-boil the eggs
- Check mackerel for bones
- Preheat oven to 190°C/375°F/Gas 5
- Lay out: ingredients, mixing bowl, mixing spoon, table knife, chopping board and oven-proof dish

ALL TOGETHER NOW!

❶ Put the cream and curry powder in the bowl and mix together.

❷ ✋ Peel off the mackerel skin and discard. Then tear the flesh into bite-sized pieces and add to the bowl.

❸ Add the rice and peas. Mix.

❹ Spoon into the oven-proof dish.
Adult: Bake 15 mins until heated through.

❺ While baking, peel the eggs and chop them into pieces with a table knife.

❻ If using, tear or snip the parsley into pieces with child-safe scissors.

AND FINALLY...

Scatter egg pieces/parsley on top to serve.

NB Don't leave cooked rice lying around. Bacteria can grow on it that isn't killed by reheating. If not using straight away, cool in running water, cover and put in the fridge.

SERVES
2–4

ACTIVITY
25

OVEN
15

Your child's schemas
(see pages 26–29)
- Transforming
- Transporting
- Rotating

Main tasks & skills
- Mixing
- Spooning
- Tearing
- Chopping

Allergy information

Egg	Leave off eggs
Dairy	Use dairy-free cream
Gluten	Not applicable
Nut	Check labels for potential contamination

Snack time

Some bits and pieces for the mid-morning and mid-afternoon munchies. Portion sizes are intentionally small to make it easier for little chefs, but you can double or even triple amounts if you are cooking for a crowd.

Savoury

 **EASY PEASY**

Nachos **54**
Pitta chips **55**
Tzatziki **56**

BUDDING COOK

Egg-free arancini **57**
Cheese straws **58**
Courgette & carrot bites **59**

 **CONFIDENT CHEF**

Breadsticks **60**
Cheesy biscuits **61**
Guacamole **62**

Sweet

EASY PEASY

Banana & cherry flapjacks **63**
Chocolate biscuit cake **64**
Egg-free cookies **65**
Chocolate fork biscuits **66**
Lemon yoghurt cake **67**
Melting moments **68**
Traditional shortbread **69**

BUDDING COOK

Banana & peanut butter cakes **70**
Chocolate cake squares **71**
Carrot cakes **72**

 **CONFIDENT CHEF**

Mini scones **73**

Nachos

Try to find unsalted or lightly salted chips, or better still, make your own by cutting or tearing tortilla wraps and baking them for about five minutes in a hot oven.

SERVES
4

 ACTIVITY
20

 OVEN
18

Your child's schemas
(see pages 26–29)
• Transporting   • Enveloping
• Connecting

Main tasks & skills
• Constructing   • Mashing
• Scooping   • Squeezing

Allergy information

Egg	Not applicable
Dairy	Swap cheese for drained, washed black beans
Gluten	Check tortilla chips label
Nut	Check labels for potential contamination

WHAT YOU NEED
+ 85 g tortilla chips
+ 100 g (1 cup) cheddar cheese
+ 6 tbsp tomato salsa (ready-made or recipe on page 83)
+ 1 avocado
+ ¼ small lime

PARENT PREP
+ Preheat oven to 190°C/375°F/Gas 5
+ Grate cheese
+ Cut around avocado lengthways and pull apart. Leave stone in and rub a little lime juice on flesh to stop it going brown
+ Lay out: ingredients, mixing bowl, fork or potato masher, tablespoon and oven-proof dish

ALL TOGETHER NOW!

❶ Spread half the tortilla chips in the oven-proof dish.

❷ Spoon dollops of tomato salsa onto the chips.

❸ Sprinkle over half the grated cheese.

❹ Layer the other half of the chips on top, followed by the rest of the cheese. **Adult:** Bake in the oven for 18 minutes, and while cooking…

❺ Use the tablespoon to scoop out the flesh from the avocado into the bowl. Discard the stone. Then mash the flesh with a fork or masher.

❻ Squeeze over the juice from the lime quarter and mix.

AND FINALLY…

Serve with mashed avocado on the side or dolloped on top.

Pitta chips

This is an easy, quick snack to just serve plain, but these chips are also great to have with either a dip or a bowl of delicious, warming soup.

WHAT YOU NEED
+ 2 pittas
+ 2 tsp of dried mixed herbs
+ 1 tbsp olive oil

PARENT PREP
+ Preheat oven to 200°C/390°F/Gas 6
+ Lay out: ingredients, child-safe scissors (optional) and baking tray

VARIATIONS
Leftover baked potato skins, tortillas, thinly sliced carrots, parsnips or aubergines

ALL TOGETHER NOW!

❶ Open the pittas and cut or tear them into 2-cm pieces.

❷ Put the pitta pieces onto the tray.

❸ Take a pinch of herbs and sprinkle them over the pitta pieces.

❹ Drizzle over the olive oil.

❺ Mix, using hands or a spoon, to coat pitta pieces with oil and herbs.

AND FINALLY...

Bake in the oven for 10 minutes until light brown and crispy.

SERVES
2–4

ACTIVITY
10

OVEN
10

Your child's schemas
(see pages 26–29)
• Transporting   • Connecting
• Trajectory

Main tasks & skills
• Tearing   • Mixing
• Sprinkling

Allergy information

Egg	Not applicable
Dairy	Not applicable
Gluten	Use gluten-free pittas
Nut	Check labels for potential contamination

Tzatziki

Also known as a 'cucumber dip', this mild and simple version of the traditional Greek dish is perfect for little chefs to create all by themselves.

SERVES

2–4

ACTIVITY

10

Your child's schemas
(see pages 26–29)
• Rotating
• Trajectory

Main tasks & skills
• Spooning   • Tearing
• Squeezing   • Mixing

Allergy information

Egg	Not applicable
Dairy	Use dairy-free yoghurt
Gluten	Not applicable
Nut	Check labels for potential contamination

WHAT YOU NEED
✦ 150 g (1 cup) cucumber
✦ 120 ml (½ cup) Greek yoghurt
✦ ½ tsp olive oil
✦ ¼ small lemon
✦ 4 fresh mint leaves (optional)

PARENT PREP
✦ Grate cucumber
✦ Lay out: ingredients, bowl and mixing spoon

ALL TOGETHER NOW!

❶ Put the grated cucumber and yoghurt into the bowl.

❷ Squeeze on the juice from the lemon quarter.

❸ Add the oil.

❹ If you are using mint, tear the leaves into little pieces and add to the bowl.

❺ Mix all the ingredients together.

AND FINALLY...

Serve with pitta chips (see page 55) or breadsticks (see page 60).

Egg-free arancini

These make a fun snack or light lunch and are a good baby-led weaning dish for a younger sibling. This recipe uses broccoli, but you can use any mashable vegetable.

WHAT YOU NEED

- ◆ 50 g (¼ cup) rice
- ◆ 50 g (about 2 'trees') broccoli
- ◆ 30 g (⅓ cup) cheddar cheese
- ◆ 3 tbsp cream cheese
- ◆ 25 g (½ cup) fresh breadcrumbs

PARENT PREP

- ◆ Preheat oven to 200°C/390°F/Gas 6
- ◆ Cook rice or use 125 g (1 cup) leftover cooked rice
- ◆ Cook broccoli until soft, or use leftovers
- ◆ Grate cheddar cheese. If you have a handled grater, children can help
- ◆ Lay out: ingredients, chopping board, fork or masher, spoon, mixing bowl, plate and baking tray

ALL TOGETHER NOW!

❶ Put the broccoli into the bowl and mash.

❷ Add rice, cheddar cheese and cream cheese to the bowl and mix.

❸ ✋ Squish everything together to form balls. If it won't combine, add more cream cheese.

❹ Put the breadcrumbs onto the plate.

❺ Put each ball onto the plate and bury it with breadcrumbs until fully coated.

❻ Place on the baking tray.

AND FINALLY...

Bake for 20 minutes.

NB Never leave cooked rice lying around because bacteria can grow on it that isn't killed by reheating. If not using straight away, cool in running cold water, cover and put into the fridge.

MAKES
8–10

ACTIVITY
25

OVEN
20

Your child's schemas
(see pages 26–29)
- Transporting
- Enveloping
- Transforming

Main tasks & skills
- Mashing
- Coating
- Sculpting

Allergy information

Egg	Not applicable
Dairy	Avoid
Gluten	Use gluten-free breadcrumbs
Nut	Check labels for potential contamination

Cheese straws

These two-ingredient cheese straws get demolished within minutes in our house. They also work with other toppings such as poppy seeds or parmesan.

MAKES

6

ACTIVITY
15

OVEN
15

Your child's schemas
(see pages 26–29)
• Transporting • Enveloping

Main tasks & skills
• Sprinkling • Cutting
• Squishing • Twisting

Allergy information

Egg	Not applicable
Dairy	Swap cheese for poppy or sesame seeds, check shop-bought puff pastry
Gluten	Use gluten-free puff pastry
Nut	Check labels for potential contamination

WHAT YOU NEED
✦ 130 g ready-rolled puff pastry sheet
✦ 40 g (½ cup) cheddar cheese

PARENT PREP
✦ Preheat oven to 220°C/425°F/Gas 7
✦ Finely grate the cheese
✦ Lay out: ingredients, table knife, chopping board, rolling pin (optional) and baking tray

ALL TOGETHER NOW!

❶ Put the ready-rolled pastry on the board.

❷ Sprinkle cheese all over the pastry.

❸ Squish the cheese into the pastry with the palm of the hand and/or roll it in with the rolling pin.

❹ Use the table knife to cut the pastry into 1.5-cm strips.

❺ Hold one end of each strip while turning the other end until you get 4 or 5 twists.

❻ Put on the baking tray and sprinkle any cheese that fell off while twisting back onto the straws.

AND FINALLY…

Bake in the oven for 12–15 minutes until golden brown. Leave to cool on the tray before serving or storing in a tin.

Courgette & carrot bites

This is a mini frittata-muffin hybrid, which is yummy and versatile for breakfasts, snacks, lunches, lunchboxes or to take on a picnic.

WHAT YOU NEED

- ½ tbsp olive oil
- 2 eggs
- ½ carrot
- ½ courgette
- 45 g (⅓ cup) self-raising flour
- 50 g (½ cup) cheddar cheese
- 1–2 rashers bacon (optional)

PARENT PREP

- Preheat oven to 190°C/375°F/Gas 5
- Grate courgette, carrot and cheese. If you have a handled grater, your toddler could help
- If using, fry bacon rashers.
- Lay out: ingredients, pastry brush, cupcake tray, large bowl, fork, mixing spoon and 2 tablespoons

ALL TOGETHER NOW!

❶ Use the pastry brush to paint oil all over the cupcake tray.

❷ Break the eggs into the bowl and whisk with a fork until mixture turns yellow.

❸ Add the flour, grated courgette, carrot and cheese. Mix everything together.

❹ If using, tear up the bacon rashers into little pieces and add to the bowl. Mix everything again.

❺ Use 2 spoons to spoon and scrape 1 heaped spoonful of mixture into each cupcake hole in the tray.

AND FINALLY…

Bake in the oven for 15 minutes, until firm and golden.

MAKES **8**

ACTIVITY **20**

OVEN **15**

Your child's schemas
(see pages 26–29)
- Rotating
- Enveloping
- Containing

Main tasks & skills
- Painting
- Spooning
- Mixing

Allergy information

Egg	Avoid
Dairy	Leave off cheese
Gluten	Use gluten-free flour
Nut	Check labels for potential contamination

Breadsticks

Breadsticks are my children's number-one snack of choice, especially with a tasty dip. Bake as sticks, or have fun sculpting shapes such as snails, letters and circles.

MAKES
6–8

ACTIVITY
20

OVEN
15

Your child's schemas
(see pages 26–29)
• Transporting • Transforming
• Enveloping

Main tasks & skills
• Mixing   • Sculpting
• Squishing   • Painting

Allergy information

Egg	Not applicable
Dairy	Use dairy-free milk
Gluten	Use gluten-free flour
Nut	Check labels for potential contamination

WHAT YOU NEED
- 90 g (⅔ cup) self-raising flour
- ⅛ tsp salt
- 60 ml (¼ cup) milk
- 1 tbsp plain flour for dusting
- 1–2 tbsp olive oil

PARENT PREP
- Preheat oven to 220°C/425°F/Gas 7
- Lay out: ingredients, mixing bowl, mixing spoon, board, baking tray and pastry brush

ALL TOGETHER NOW!

❶ Put the flour, salt and milk into the bowl and mix until they come together.

❷ Dust the plain flour onto the board and tip the mixture onto it.

❸ Squish and squash the mixture on the board until you get a smooth dough.

❹ Take a small chunk of dough and roll it out with flat hands until you get a long, thin worm shape. Repeat.

❺ Use the pastry brush to paint oil all over the tray.

❻ Put the dough sticks onto the tray and brush more oil on the tops.

AND FINALLY...

Bake in the oven for 10–15 minutes (depending on the thickness of the sticks), until they turn golden brown.

Cheesy biscuits

I said don't worry about making things dinner-party worthy, but I do serve these as party nibbles. I love seeing surprised friends' faces when I tell them who made them.

WHAT YOU NEED
- 50 g (⅓ cup) self-raising flour, plus some for dusting
- 40 g butter
- 40 g (½ cup) parmesan cheese
- 10 g (2 tbsp) cheddar cheese
- ½ tbsp water

PARENT PREP
- Preheat oven to 180°C/350°F/Gas 4
- Grate parmesan and cheddar
- Take butter out of the fridge at least an hour beforehand, to soften
- Lay out: ingredients, mixing bowl, fork, mat/board, rolling pin, cookie cutter (approx 45 mm) and lined baking tray

ALL TOGETHER NOW!

1 Mush the cheese into the butter with a fork.

2 Mix in the self-raising flour.

3 🖐 Sprinkle over the water and squeeze the mixture together with hands until you have a ball of dough.

4 Dust the flour all over the mat/board and rolling pin to prevent sticking.

5 Roll out the dough to about 4 mm thick.

6 Cut out the shapes with a cookie cutter and place them on the baking tray.

AND FINALLY...

Bake for 8–10 minutes until golden brown.

MAKES
12

ACTIVITY
25

OVEN
10

Your child's schemas
(see pages 26–29)
- Transforming
- Transporting

Main tasks & skills
- Mushing
- Mixing
- Squishing
- Rolling

Allergy information

Egg	Not applicable
Dairy	Avoid
Gluten	Use gluten-free flour
Nut	Check labels for potential contamination

Guacamole

A great recipe for talking about colours (purple, green and red) and textures (hard avocado stone, soft avocado flesh, smooth tomato skin and rough avocado skin).

SERVES

3–4

ACTIVITY

15

Your child's schemas
(see pages 26–29)
• Transforming
• Rotating

Main tasks & skills
• Mashing
• Squeezing
• Cutting
• Mixing

Allergy information

Egg	Not applicable
Dairy	Not applicable
Gluten	Not applicable
Nut	Check labels for potential contamination

WHAT YOU NEED
✦ 1 ripe avocado
✦ 2 cherry tomatoes
✦ 1 small garlic clove
✦ ¼ small lime
✦ Tiny pinch salt (optional)

PARENT PREP
✦ Cut vertically around avocado so your child can pull it open
✦ Lay out: ingredients; mixing bowl, metal spoon, fork or potato masher, table knife, chopping board, garlic press

ALL TOGETHER NOW!

❶ Spoon out the avocado flesh into the bowl and mash it with a fork or masher. Discard the stone.

❷ Squeeze over the juice from the lime quarter and mix into the avocado.

❸ Use the table knife to cut the tomatoes in half.

❹ Use the table knife to cut the garlic clove in half, then peel. Discard the peel.

❺ Squash the cherry tomatoes and garlic through the garlic press into the bowl.

❻ Sprinkle on the salt (optional). Mix thoroughly.

AND FINALLY...

Serve with nachos (page 54), pitta chips (page 55), breadsticks (page 60) or carrot or cucumber sticks.

Banana & cherry flapjacks

Easy, everything-into-the-bowl flapjacks. If you want a low-sugar version, you can leave out the syrup/honey because the banana binds them.

WHAT YOU NEED

+ ½ banana
+ 3 tbsp vegetable oil
+ 1 tbsp golden syrup or honey
+ 100 g (1 cup) oats
+ 10 glacé cherries

PARENT PREP

+ Preheat oven to 180°C/350°F/Gas 4
+ Lay out: ingredients, mixing bowl, fork or potato masher, table spoon and 20-cm (1-lb/450-g) loaf tin

ALL TOGETHER NOW!

1 Peel and put the banana in the bowl. Mash with a fork or a masher.

2 Add the oil and golden syrup. Mix.

3 Count out the 10 cherries, then tear or squish them into about 4 pieces. Add them to the bowl.

4 Add the oats and mix again.

5 Spoon the mixture into the loaf tin.

6 Spread out and pat down with a spoon or hands until it is level-ish.

AND FINALLY…

Bake in the oven for 30 minutes. Cut into portions while warm, then leave to cool in the tin before removing.

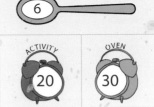

MAKES 6

ACTIVITY 20

OVEN 30

Your child's schemas
(see pages 26–29)

- Transporting
- Rotating
- Transforming

Main tasks & skills

- Mashing
- Spooning
- Tearing
- Squashing
- Counting

Allergy information

Egg	Not applicable
Dairy	Not applicable
Gluten	Oats usually okay, but check label for potential contamination
Nut	Check labels for potential contamination

Chocolate biscuit cake

Definitely not a healthy option, but this delicious no-bake cake will give the budding chef the best chocolatey fingers they've ever had the chance to lick!

MAKES
6–8

ACTIVITY **20**   CHILL **60**

Your child's schemas
(see pages 26–29)
- Transforming
- Trajectory
- Rotating
- Transporting

Main tasks & skills
- Breaking
- Pouring
- Mixing
- Squashing

Allergy information

Egg	Not applicable
Dairy	Use dairy-free spread and check the digestives label
Gluten	Use gluten-free biscuits
Nut	Check labels for potential contamination

WHAT YOU NEED
✦ 120 g (about 8) digestive biscuits
✦ 3 tbsp raisins
✦ 30 g (3 tbsp) butter
✦ 3 tbsp cocoa powder
✦ 3 tbsp golden syrup

PARENT PREP
✦ Gently melt butter, cocoa powder and golden syrup together in a pan. Transfer to a jug
✦ Lay out: remaining ingredients, 15-cm cake tin or 20-cm (1-lb/450-g) loaf tin, 2 tablespoons, mixing bowl and greaseproof paper

VARIATION
Swap digestives for any plain biscuit, cornflakes or rice crispies

ALL TOGETHER NOW!

❶ Break the digestives into about 6–8 pieces. Put them into the bowl.

❷ Add the raisins and mix them in.

❸ Pour the melted syrup mixture onto the biscuits and mix until the biscuit bits are completely covered.

❹ Use 2 spoons to spoon and scrape the mixture into the cake tin.

❺ Spread the mixture out and press down with hands to make a compressed, flat top. If the children don't like sticky hands, put the greaseproof paper on before they press down.

AND FINALLY...

Cover the top with greaseproof paper and put into the fridge for at least an hour. Cut into slices to serve.

Egg-free cookies

I've used chocolate chips here, but you can make different versions: raisins with pinch of cinnamon, orange/lemon zest, thumb-print holes to fill with jam, or just plain.

WHAT YOU NEED

- 45 g butter
- ½ tbsp caster sugar
- ½ tbsp demerara sugar
- 1 tbsp Greek-style or natural yoghurt
- 65 g (½ cup) plain flour
- ⅛ tsp bicarbonate of soda
- 50 g (¼ cup) chocolate chips

PARENT PREP

- Take butter out of the fridge at least an hour before using, to soften
- Preheat the oven to 180°C/350°F/Gas 4
- Lay out: ingredients, mixing bowl, mixing spoon and baking tray

ALL TOGETHER NOW!

1 Squish, squash and mix the butter, sugar and yoghurt until combined.

2 Add the flour, bicarbonate of soda and chocolate chips and mix until it comes together. If the mixture is too dry, add a little more yoghurt.

3 Mould the dough into 6 balls.

4 Put on the baking tray and flatten with hands.

AND FINALLY...

Bake in the oven for 15–20 minutes until golden but still soft. Leave to cool before removing from the tray.

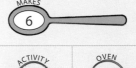

MAKES
6

ACTIVITY
20

OVEN
20

Your child's schemas
(see pages 26–29)

- Rotating
- Transforming
- Transporting

Main tasks & skills

- Squishing
- Sculpting
- Mixing
- Squashing

Allergy information

Egg	Not applicable
Dairy	Use dairy-free spread and yoghurt
Gluten	Use gluten-free flour
Nut	Check labels for potential contamination

Chocolate fork biscuits

These were the first things I made with my girls when they were about 13–14 months of age. My mum used to make them with me too.

MAKES
8

ACTIVITY
20

OVEN
9

Your child's schemas
(see pages 26–29)
• Transporting   • Transforming
• Rotating

Main tasks & skills
• Squishing   • Squashing
• Sculpting

Allergy information

Egg	Not applicable
Dairy	Use dairy-free spread
Gluten	Use gluten-free flour
Nut	Check labels for potential contamination

WHAT YOU NEED
✦ 65 g butter
✦ 2 tbsp sugar
✦ 65 g (½ cup) self-raising flour
✦ 2 tbsp cocoa powder

PARENT PREP
✦ Take butter out of the fridge at least an hour before cooking, to soften
✦ Preheat the oven to 180°C/350°F/Gas 4
✦ Lay out: ingredients, mixing bowl, mixing spoon, 2 tablespoons, cup of water, fork and baking tray

ALL TOGETHER NOW!

❶ Put the butter and sugar into the bowl and squish and stir until well combined.

❷ Add the flour and cocoa powder and mix until combined. Don't worry if mixture is dry – squish together with hands.

❸ 🖐 Take out walnut-sized lumps and shape them into balls. Put the balls onto the tray – spaced out because they will spread.

❹ Lightly press the top of each ball with a fork. If the mixture sticks to the fork, dip it into the cup of water in between each ball.

AND FINALLY...

Bake in the oven for 9 minutes. Leave to cool on the tray.

Lemon yoghurt cake

Yoghurt is a binding agent, so this is a good cake to make egg-free; great for toddlers who like to sneak a lick of cake batter or who haven't yet mastered breaking eggs.

WHAT YOU NEED

- 160 g (⅔ cup) natural or Greek-style yoghurt
- 125 g (1 cup) self-raising flour
- ¼ tsp bicarbonate of soda
- 60 ml (¼ cup) vegetable oil
- 75 g (⅓ cup) sugar
- ½ lemon
- 3 tbsp icing sugar (optional)

PARENT PREP

- Preheat oven to 160°C/320°F/Gas 3
- Take zest off lemon half and set aside
- Lay out: ingredients, mixing bowl, lemon squeezer (optional), hand whisk, 18-cm lined cake tin, spatula and, if icing, a small mixing bowl and teaspoon

ALL TOGETHER NOW!

❶ Put the yoghurt, oil, flour, bicarbonate of soda, sugar and lemon zest into the bowl.

❷ Squeeze the juice from the lemon half and add to the bowl.

❸ Whisk until ingredients are combined.

❹ Tip the batter into the cake tin and spread out with the spatula.

AND FINALLY...

Bake for 40–45 minutes until springy to the touch. You can serve the cake as it is or wait for it to cool to add the icing. Mix the icing sugar with 1–2 tsp water. Use a spoon to drizzle the icing over the top; the crazier the pattern, the better.

MAKES **1**

 ACTIVITY **20**

 OVEN **45**

Your child's schemas
(see pages 26–29)
- Rotating
- Trajectory

Main tasks & skills
- Squeezing
- Mixing
- Scraping
- Decorating

Allergy information

Egg	Not applicable
Dairy	Use dairy-free yoghurt
Gluten	Use gluten-free flour
Nut	Check labels for potential contamination

Melting moments

This was my granny's favourite biscuit recipe. Hers included some beaten egg to make them fluffier, but as they work well without, I leave it out when cooking with toddlers.

MAKES
6–8

ACTIVITY
25

OVEN
18

Your child's schemas
(see pages 26–29)
- Transporting
- Transforming
- Rotating
- Trajectory

Main tasks & skills
- Bashing
- Mixing
- Sculpting
- Coating

Allergy information

Egg	Not applicable
Dairy	Use dairy-free spread
Gluten	Use gluten-free cornflakes and flour
Nut	Check labels for potential contamination

WHAT YOU NEED
- 50 g butter
- 2 tbsp sugar
- ¼ tsp vanilla extract
- 1 tsp water
- 65 g (½ cup) self-raising flour
- 1 adult handful (½ cup) cornflakes

PARENT PREP
- Take butter out of the fridge at least an hour before cooking, to soften
- Put cornflakes into a freezer bag
- Preheat the oven to 180°C/350°F/Gas 4
- Lay out: ingredients, small plate, rolling pin (or other bashing implement), mixing bowl, mixing spoon, bowl of water and baking tray

ALL TOGETHER NOW!

❶ Hold one end of the freezer bag while your child bashes it with the rolling pin to crush the cornflakes.

❷ Tip the cornflakes onto a plate. Set aside.

❸ Put the butter, sugar, vanilla and water into a large bowl and mix until combined.

❹ Add the flour and mix again until combined. If the mix is too dry to combine, add ½ tsp more water.

❺  Dip hands into a bowl of water, then take a lump of the mixture and make a walnut-sized ball.

❻ Roll each ball in crushed cornflakes and place on the tray.

AND FINALLY...

Bake for 18 minutes. Leave to cool for at least 5 minutes on the tray before removing.

Traditional shortbread

This classic recipe has many versions and ways of making it. This method is fun – a bit like making 'sand' and then building a sandcastle with it.

WHAT YOU NEED

+ 125 g butter, plus ½ tsp for greasing
+ 60 g (¼ cup) brown sugar
+ 180 g (1¼ cups) plain flour

PARENT PREP

+ Take butter out of fridge at least an hour before using, to soften
+ Preheat oven to 170°C/340°F/Gas 3
+ Lay out: ingredients, 20-cm (1-lb or 450-g) loaf tin, mixing bowl, tablespoon, mixing spoon and fork

ALL TOGETHER NOW!

❶ Rub ½ tsp of butter all over the cake tin to grease it. Set aside.

❷ Put the butter and sugar into the bowl and squish and stir with a wooden spoon until they are well combined.

❸ Mix in the flour until it is just combined. Don't worry if it looks crumbly.

❹ Put the mixture into the tin. Spread and pat it down as if you were making a sand castle.

❺ Lightly prick the dough all over with the fork.

AND FINALLY...

Bake in the oven for 40 minutes until light brown. Cut into portions while still warm in the tin and if you want to be strictly traditional, sprinkle some caster sugar on top. Then leave to cool before removing.

MAKES **8**

 ACTIVITY **20**   OVEN **40**

Your child's schemas
(see pages 26–29)
• Enveloping   • Transforming
• Rotating

Main tasks & skills
• Rubbing   • Patting
• Mixing   • Pricking

Allergy information

Egg	Not applicable
Dairy	Use dairy-free spread
Gluten	Use gluten-free flour
Nut	Check labels for potential contamination

Banana & peanut butter cakes

My children don't think a cake is a cake unless it has icing and sprinkles, but these ones are great without icing if you want a healthier option.

MAKES
8

ACTIVITY
20

OVEN
20

Your child's schemas
(see pages 26–29)
- Transforming
- Containing
- Rotating

Main tasks & skills
- Counting
- Mashing
- Whisking
- Spooning

Allergy information

Egg	Avoid
Dairy	Use dairy-free milk or water and check peanut-butter label
Gluten	Use gluten-free flour
Nut	Swap peanut butter for 50 ml veg oil and 100 g choc chips. Leave off icing. Check labels for potential contamination

WHAT YOU NEED
- 1 ripe banana
- 2 tbsp light-brown sugar (optional)
- 1 egg
- 50 ml milk
- 125 g (1 cup) self-raising flour
- 70 g (⅓ cup) chunky peanut butter

For the icing:
- 65 g (½ cup) icing sugar
- 1 tbsp peanut butter
- 1–2 tbsp milk

PARENT PREP
- Preheat oven to 180°C/350°F/Gas 4
- Lay out: ingredients, cupcake tray, 8 cupcake cases, mixing bowl, whisk, mixing spoon, fork or potato masher and 2 tablespoons

ALL TOGETHER NOW!

❶ Count the cupcake cases into a tray and set aside.

❷ Put the banana and peanut butter into the mixing bowl and mash them together with a fork or potato masher.

❸ Add the sugar, egg and milk – and whisk.

❹ Add flour and stir until combined.

❺ Spoon the mixture into the cases until each is two-thirds full.

AND FINALLY…

Bake for 15–20 minutes until springy to the touch. If you are adding icing, leave the cakes to cool, then mix the icing ingredients and dollop onto the tops.

Chocolate cake squares

Great for little chefs because it's just putting everything into the bowl and whisking. I've made it square for easier cutting, but it works just as well round.

WHAT YOU NEED

- 160 g (1¼ cups) self-raising flour
- 4 tbsp cocoa powder
- 90 g (⅓ cup) sugar
- ¼ tsp salt
- 100 ml (⅓ cup) milk
- 60 ml (¼ cup) vegetable oil, plus a little for greasing
- 2 eggs
- 1 tsp vanilla extract
- 100 ml (½ cup) water
- 3 heaped tbsp chocolate hazelnut spread

PARENT PREP

- Preheat oven to 180°C/350°F/Gas 4
- Lay out: ingredients, large mixing bowl, hand whisk, pastry brush, 20-cm square cake tin, spatula, cooling rack, table knife and tablespoon

ALL TOGETHER NOW!

❶ Use the pastry brush to paint a little oil over the cake tin to grease it.

❷ Put all the ingredients except for the chocolate spread into the bowl.

❸ Mix well with the hand whisk.

❹ Pour the mixture into the cake tin.
   Adult: Bake in oven for 25 minutes until the cake is springy to the touch. Cool on a cooling rack.

❺ Dollop 3 generous spoonfuls of chocolate spread onto the cooled cake and spread it evenly. Use a table knife to cut the cake into small squares to serve.

MAKES **20**

ACTIVITY **20**

OVEN **25**

Your child's schemas
(see pages 26–29)
- Transforming
- Trajectory
- Rotating

Main tasks & skills
- Painting
- Pouring
- Whisking

Allergy information

Egg	Leave out
Dairy	Use dairy-free milk and spread top with jam
Gluten	Use gluten-free flour
Nut	Ice with chocolate frosting. Check labels for potential contamination

Carrot cakes

This is an easy carrot-cake mix that can be made as little individual cakes or as one large cake. If you want to add decoration add a yoghurt/cream-cheese topping.

MAKES
6

ACTIVITY
20

OVEN
20

Your child's schemas
(see pages 26–29)
- Containing
- Rotating
- Transforming

Main tasks & skills
- Mixing
- Spooning
- Counting

Allergy information

Egg	Use 2 tbsp natural yoghurt
Dairy	Don't add topping
Gluten	Use gluten-free flour
Nut	Check labels for potential contamination

WHAT YOU NEED
- 1 egg
- 10 ml (2 tsp) orange juice
- 3 tbsp vegetable oil
- 3 tbsp light muscovado sugar
- 60 g (½ cup) self-raising flour
- 60 g (1 medium) carrot
- ⅛ tsp ground cinnamon

For the optional topping:
- 3 tbsp cream cheese
- 1½ tbsp natural yoghurt

PARENT PREP
- Preheat oven to 180°C/350°F/Gas 4
- Grate carrot
- Lay out: ingredients, mixing bowl, fork, mixing spoon, 2 tablespoons, cupcake tray and 6 cases

ALL TOGETHER NOW!

❶ Break the egg into a bowl.

❷ Add the oil and orange juice and whisk with a fork.

❸ Add the flour, sugar, cinnamon and carrot. Mix until they are combined.

❹ Count the cupcake cases into the tray.

❺ Spoon and scrape the mixture into the cases until they are two-thirds full.

AND FINALLY…

Bake in the oven for 18–20 minutes until the top is firm and springy. If you want to add topping, mix together the cream cheese and yoghurt and dollop on once cooled. If you are not eating straight away, store without the topping.

Mini scones

This is a variation on my husband's gran's scone recipe. She used to make one giant scone, cut into slices to serve. These mini versions make a great tea-time treat or snack.

WHAT YOU NEED
+ 35 g butter
+ 130 g (1 cup) self-raising flour
+ ½ tbsp sugar
+ Tiny pinch salt
+ 35 g (¼ cup) currants
+ 60 ml (¼ cup) milk
+ 1 tbsp milk for brushing tops

PARENT PREP
+ Preheat oven to 190°C/375°F/Gas 5
+ Lay out: ingredients, mixing bowl, mixing spoon, 48-mm round cookie cutter, pastry brush, baking tray, table knife and chopping board

ALL TOGETHER NOW!

❶ Cut the butter into little pieces.

❷ Put the flour and butter pieces into the bowl. Rub the butter into the flour using fingertips until it looks like breadcrumbs.

❸ Add the sugar, currants and a pinch of salt and mix.

❹ Add the milk and mix. Bring the mixture together with hands until you have a lump of dough.

❺ Tip onto the board. Flatten out the dough with hands to 1.5 cm thick.

❻ Cut out dough circles with a cutter. Put the shapes on the baking tray and paint the tops with milk using a pastry brush.

AND FINALLY…

Bake in oven for 15 minutes until light brown. If you're making a single scone, bake for an extra 5 minutes.

MAKES
8

 ACTIVITY
25

 OVEN
15

Your child's schemas
(see pages 26–29)
• Transforming
• Transporting

Main tasks & skills
• Tickling
• Squishing
• Mixing
• Painting

Allergy information

Egg	Not applicable
Dairy	Use dairy-free spread and milk
Gluten	Use gluten-free flour
Nut	Check labels for potential contamination

Lunch for us

Speaking from experience, getting food on the table with a needy toddler hanging off your legs or balanced on one hip is not easy. Doing quick and simple recipes like these together can be easier and a lot more fun!

Curried chicken wraps

This is a fun recipe for using up leftover chicken and exploring tastes like bitterness (lime), sweetness (mango chutney) and spiciness (curry powder).

MAKES

2

ACTIVITY

15

Your child's schemas
(see pages 26–29)
- Rotating
- Enveloping
- Transporting

Main tasks & skills
- Tearing
- Squeezing
- Mixing
- Spreading
- Wrapping

Allergy information

Egg	Use egg-free mayo
Dairy	Use dairy-free yoghurt. Check the mayo label
Gluten	Use gluten-free wraps
Nut	Check labels for potential contamination

WHAT YOU NEED
- 120 g (1 cup) cooked chicken
- 2 tbsp Greek-style yoghurt
- 2 tbsp mayonnaise
- ¼ level tsp mild curry powder
- 1½ tsp mango chutney
- ¼ small lime
- 2 ready-made wraps

PARENT PREP
- Lay out: ingredients, mixing bowl, 2 tablespoons, table knife, chopping board and kitchen foil (optional)

ALL TOGETHER NOW!

❶ Tear the chicken into smallish pieces and put them into the mixing bowl.

❷ Add the yoghurt, mayonnaise, curry powder and mango chutney to the bowl.

❸ Squeeze the juice from the lime quarter into the bowl. Mix with a spoon until combined.

❹ Spoon half the mixture onto the wrap and spread it out.

❺ Roll up the wrap and cut in half with a table knife. Repeat with the other wrap. If you are not eating them straight away, wrap them in kitchen-foil parcels.

Ham & mushroom pizza

This is my personal-favourite pizza topping, but let them choose their own. Other good instant bases include English muffins, flatbread and pittas.

WHAT YOU NEED

+ 1 flour tortilla
+ 1 tbsp ready-made tomato pasta sauce
+ 50 g (⅓ cup) cooked ham
+ 50 g (⅔ cup) mushrooms
+ 100 g (½ cup) fresh mozzarella
+ 2 large basil leaves (optional)
+ 1 tbsp olive oil

PARENT PREP

+ Preheat oven to 200°C/390°F/Gas 6
+ Put olive oil in a saucer
+ Lay out: ingredients, baking tray and 2 tablespoons

ALL TOGETHER NOW!

❶ Put the tortilla onto the tray. Spoon the tomato sauce onto the tortilla and spread it out with the back of a spoon.

❷ Tear the ham and mushrooms into small pieces. Scatter them on top of the tortilla.

❸ Tear the mozzarella and basil leaves and scatter on the tortilla.

❹ Gently tip the saucer to drizzle the olive oil over the top.

AND FINALLY…

Bake in the oven for 8 minutes.

NB It's best to eat the pizza straight from the oven, so if you want to prepare it in advance, cover and put it in the fridge until you are ready to cook.

MAKES
1

ACTIVITY
15

OVEN
8

Your child's schemas
(see pages 26–29)
• Connecting
• Transporting

Main tasks & skills
• Spreading   • Constructing
• Tearing

Allergy information

Egg	Not applicable
Dairy	Avoid
Gluten	Use gluten-free tortilla
Nut	Check labels for potential contamination

Pirate treasure salad

An easy way to get children to explore fruit and veg. My three-year-old named it Pirate Treasure Salad and likes to 'dig for treasure' to find the bits she likes best.

SERVES
2–3

ACTIVITY
20

Your child's schemas
(see pages 26–29)
• Connecting
• Transporting

Main tasks & skills
• Counting   • Mixing
• Constructing   • Shaking

Allergy information

Egg	Not applicable
Dairy	Leave out mozzarella
Gluten	Leave out croutons
Nut	Check labels for potential contamination

WHAT YOU NEED

✦ 3 cherry tomatoes (rubies)
✦ 1 small carrot (fire opals)
✦ 3 tbsp tinned sweetcorn kernels (gold)
✦ 100 g (3 adult handfuls) mixed lettuce leaves
✦ 3 tbsp blueberries (sapphires)
✦ 5 green grapes (emeralds)
✦ 50 g fresh mozzarella (moonstones)
✦ 3 tbsp croutons (diamonds)
✦ Dressing: 2 tbsp olive oil, ½ tsp mustard, ½ tbsp honey, ½ tsp balsamic vinegar

PARENT PREP

✦ Peel and chop carrot
✦ Lay out: ingredients, chopping board, table knife, large mixing bowl, 2 tablespoons and empty jamjar with lid

ALL TOGETHER NOW!

❶ Use the table knife to chop the tomatoes into quarters and the grapes into halves.

❷ Tear the mozzarella into small pieces.

❸ Put the lettuce into the bowl.

❹ Let the children loose on the ingredients – tasting everything, adding what they want and choosing how much.

❺ Mix up the salad with spoons.

❻ Put the dressing ingredients into the jamjar. Put the lid on tightly and shake, shake, shake.

AND FINALLY…

Put on the table and let your pirates dig for treasure!

Smoked mackerel pâté

This is a fun recipe for children who like to get their hands into mixtures. But if they don't like getting their hands messy, use a fork to mush the fish.

WHAT YOU NEED

- 170 g (approx 2 fillets) boneless smoked mackerel
- 4 tbsp cream cheese
- 2 tbsp cream
- ½ tsp tomato paste
- ⅛ tsp paprika
- ¼ small lemon

PARENT PREP

- Check for fish bones
- Lay out: ingredients, mixing bowl, 2 tablespoons, fork and pot or container with lid

VARIATION

You can use a tin of boneless salmon to make salmon pâté

ALL TOGETHER NOW!

1 Pull the skin off the mackerel and discard it. Put the flesh into the bowl.

2 Squish and squash the mackerel with hands until it is mushy.

3 Add the cream cheese, cream, tomato paste and paprika.

4 Squeeze the lemon quarter so that the juice goes into the bowl. Mix until all the ingredients are combined.

5 Spoon the mixture into a container.

AND FINALLY...

Even if you've bought boneless fish and checked it for bones before using, check again before spreading onto cold toast or crackers to serve. Keep covered in the fridge if you are not eating straight away.

SERVES 4

ACTIVITY 20

Your child's schemas
(see pages 26–29)
- Enveloping
- Transforming

Main tasks & skills
- Mushing
- Squishing
- Mixing
- Squeezing
- Spooning

Allergy information

Egg	Not applicable
Dairy	Avoid
Gluten	Not applicable
Nut	Check labels for potential contamination

Tuna mayo pitta pockets

These are a lunchtime favourite in our house. Prepare them in advance and then warm just before eating. They are also good uncooked for picnics.

MAKES
4

ACTIVITY
15

OVEN
5

Your child's schemas
(see pages 26–29)
- Containing
- Enveloping
- Transforming

Main tasks & skills
- Mushing
- Stuffing
- Mixing

Allergy information

Egg	Leave out mayo
Dairy	Leave out cheese and check mayo label
Gluten	Use gluten-free pittas
Nut	Check labels for potential contamination

WHAT YOU NEED
- 200 g (1 cup) tinned tuna
- 3 tbsp mayonnaise
- 3 tbsp tinned sweetcorn
- 70 g (⅔ cup) cheddar cheese
- 4 pitta halves

PARENT PREP
- Open tuna and sweetcorn tins and drain off liquid
- Grate cheddar cheese, or if you have a handled grater let your child do it
- Preheat oven to 180°C/350°F/Gas 4
- Lay out: ingredients, mixing bowl, 2 tablespoons, fork and baking tray

ALL TOGETHER NOW!

❶ Scrape the tuna into the mixing bowl.

❷ Spoon mayonnaise into the mixing bowl and mush into the tuna with hands or a fork.

❸ Add the sweetcorn and mix together.

❹ Spoon or use hands to put 2 spoonfuls of tuna mix into each pitta half.

❺ Use hands to shove a handful of grated cheese inside each pitta half.

❻ Put on the baking tray.

AND FINALLY...

Warm in the oven for 5 minutes.
Eat straight away.

Chicken bread baskets

These little baskets look and taste great. You can serve them with a salad for lunch, but they also make great party food for adults and children alike.

WHAT YOU NEED
+ 1 tbsp olive oil
+ 4 slices bread
+ 90 g (¾ cup) cooked chicken
+ 3 tbsp mayonnaise
+ 1 tsp tarragon/parsley
+ ½ tsp mustard

PARENT PREP
+ Chop tarragon/parsley or use dried
+ Preheat oven to 180°C/350°F/Gas 4
+ Lay out: ingredients: cupcake tray, rolling pin (optional), pastry brush, 68-mm round cookie cutter, mixing bowl, tablespoon, 2 teaspoons and cooling rack

VARIATION
The smoked mackerel pâté recipe (page 79) also makes a good filling

ALL TOGETHER NOW!

❶ Cut 2 circles of bread from each slice with a cookie cutter, making 8 circles in total.

❷ Squash each bread circle with hands or roll until it is flat. Paint each circle with oil using the pastry brush.

❸ Place circles into the cupcake tray and press down to make basket shapes.
Adult: Bake baskets for 10 minutes, until they are light brown and crisp. Remove from the tray and cool on a cooling rack.

❹ While the bread baskets are cooking/ cooling, tear up the chicken.

❺ Put chicken, mayonnaise, tarragon and mustard into mixing bowl and mix. When baskets are cold, spoon the mixture in.

AND FINALLY...

Serve and eat within an hour, otherwise the baskets will go soggy.

MAKES
8

 ACTIVITY **30**

 OVEN **10**

Your child's schemas
(see pages 26–29)
• Containing   • Transporting
• Connecting

Main tasks & skills
• Cutting   • Painting
• Squashing   • Spooning

Allergy information
Egg	Make with mackerel paté filling (page 79)
Dairy	Check mayo label
Gluten	Gluten-free bread
Nut	Check labels for potential contamination

Frittata

Frittatas are great for using up leftover vegetables, especially potatoes. I just use whatever I have left over from supper the night before or the lunchtime roast.

SERVES
2–3

ACTIVITY
20

OVEN
35

Your child's schemas
(see pages 26–29)
• Enveloping
• Rotating
• Trajectory

Main tasks & skills
• Painting
• Whisking
• Chopping
• Pouring

Allergy information

Egg	Avoid
Dairy	Use dairy-free milk and leave out cheese
Gluten	Not applicable
Nut	Check labels for potential contamination

WHAT YOU NEED

+ 1 tbsp olive oil
+ 200 g (1½ cups) mixed vegetables of your choice e.g. cooked potatoes, broccoli, courgettes, peas, peppers, cooked carrots
+ 4 eggs
+ 120 ml (½ cup) milk
+ 70 g (⅔ cup) grated cheddar cheese

PARENT PREP

+ Grate cheddar cheese
+ Preheat oven to 180°C/350°F/Gas 4
+ Lay out: ingredients, oven-proof dish or pan, pastry brush, fork, large mixing bowl, chopping board and table knife

ALL TOGETHER NOW!

❶ Brush the oil all over the oven-proof dish with a pastry brush.

❷ Break the eggs into the mixing bowl. Add the milk and whisk together with a fork.

❸ Cut the vegetables into chunks with the table knife or tear them. Add to the bowl.

❹ Add the grated cheese and mix everything together with a fork.

❺ Pour the mixture into the oven-proof dish.

AND FINALLY...

Season and bake in the oven for 30–35 minutes until golden and firm.

Tomato salsa bruschetta
If your little ones are too young to chop or snip, make the salsa yourself and let them 'paint'/'decorate' the ciabatta with salsa and basil.

WHAT YOU NEED

For tomato salsa:

+ 8 cherry tomatoes
+ 1 spring onion
+ ¼ small or ⅛ large lime

For bruschetta:

+ ½ ciabatta loaf
+ 1–2 tbsp olive oil
+ basil leaves (optional)

PARENT PREP

+ Slice and toast ciabatta
+ Lay out: ingredients, table knife, chopping bowl, child-safe scissors, bowl, tablespoon and pastry brush

ALL TOGETHER NOW!

For the tomato salsa:

❶ Use the table knife to chop the tomatoes into 8 pieces and put into the bowl.

❷ Use the scissors to snip the spring onion into little pieces and add to the bowl.

❸ Squeeze over the juice of the lime quarter and mix in.

For the bruschetta:

❶ Brush the olive oil over each slice of toast.

❷ Spoon a dollop of salsa onto each slice.

❸ Tear the basil leaves into little pieces and sprinkle on top.

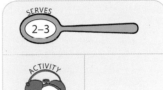

SERVES 2–3

ACTIVITY 25

Your child's schemas
(see pages 26–29)
- Connecting
- Transporting
- Enveloping

Main tasks & skills
- Chopping
- Snipping
- Painting
- Constructing

Allergy information

Egg	Not applicable
Dairy	Not applicable
Gluten	Use gluten-free ciabatta
Nut	Check labels for potential contamination

Vegetable samosas

A bit more Parent Prep than I would normally like, but lots of fun to make and great for using up small amounts of leftover veg; use whatever you've got in the fridge.

MAKES
8

ACTIVITY
35

OVEN
20

Your child's schemas
(see pages 26–29)
- Enveloping
- Containing
- Transporting
- Transforming

Main tasks & skills
- Chopping
- Painting
- Wrapping
- Changing shapes

Allergy information

Egg	Not applicable
Dairy	Fry onions in oil not butter
Gluten	Avoid
Nut	Check labels for potential contamination

WHAT YOU NEED

- 35 g (1 small) cooked potato
- 35 g (1 small) cooked carrot
- 25 g (2 tbsp) cooked green beans
- ½ small onion
- ½ tsp butter
- ½ tsp garam masala
- 25 g (3 tbsp) frozen peas
- 8 filo pastry sheets about 24 cm long
- 4 tbsp vegetable oil

PARENT PREP

- Finely chop onion, fry in the butter on medium heat until soft. Just before removing from heat, stir in garam masala
- Preheat oven to 180°C/350°F/Gas 4
- Lay out: ingredients, chopping board, table knife, mixing bowl, table spoon, pastry brush and baking tray

ALL TOGETHER NOW!

❶ Cut the cooked potato, carrot and beans into small chunks. Put into the bowl.

❷ Add the frozen peas and cooked, spiced onions to the bowl. Mix together well.

❸ Lay out one sheet of filo pasty. Brush with oil and fold lengthways, turning the square into a rectangle.

❹ Put a spoonful of the mixture in the bottom right corner.

❺ Fold the bottom left corner over the right-hand edge. Fold bottom right corner to the right edge. Keep folding until you have a triangular parcel.

❻ Brush the parcel with oil and put it on the baking tray. Repeat for each samosa.

AND FINALLY...

Bake in the oven for 15–20 minutes until golden and crisp. Serve with mango chutney.

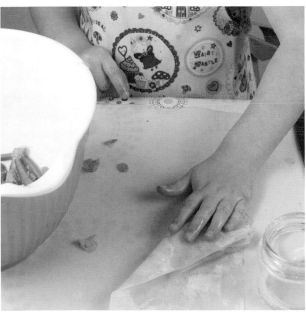

Cheese & bacon muffins

Delicious savoury muffins for breakfast, lunch or picnics. Making them in muffin cases is good for adults, but cupcake size is better for toddlers.

MAKES
9

 ACTIVITY **25** | OVEN **20**

Your child's schemas
(see pages 26–29)
• Rotating
• Containing

Main tasks & skills
• Counting
• Whisking
• Tearing
• Mixing
• Spooning

Allergy information

Egg	Avoid
Dairy	Avoid
Gluten	Use gluten-free flour
Nut	Check labels for potential contamination

WHAT YOU NEED
✦ 2 bacon rashers
✦ 125 g (1 cup) self-raising flour
✦ 75 g (¾ cup) cheddar cheese
✦ 1 small egg
✦ 50 ml (3 tbsp) milk
✦ 50 ml (3 tbsp) olive oil
✦ 50 ml (3 tbsp) tinned cream of mushroom soup

PARENT PREP
✦ Fry bacon and leave to cool
✦ Grate cheddar cheese
✦ Preheat oven to 190°C/375°F/Gas 5
✦ Lay out: ingredients, 1 cupcake tray, 9 cupcake cases, mixing bowl, mixing spoon, 2 tablespoons and fork

ALL TOGETHER NOW!

❶ Count the cupcake cases into the tray and set aside.

❷ Break the egg into the bowl. Add the milk, olive oil and mushroom soup. Whisk with a fork until everything is combined.

❸ Tear the cooked bacon rashers into little pieces and add to the bowl.

❹ Add the flour and grated cheese. Mix until everything is just combined.

❺ Spoon the mixture into the cases until about two-thirds full.

AND FINALLY...

Bake for 20 minutes until springy to the touch.

Homemade pitta bread

For perfect, fluffy pitta bread you need to spend a bit of time proving and kneading. This recipe gets you almost perfect pitta, but with speedy results.

WHAT YOU NEED

- 135 g (1 cup) wholemeal or white bread flour, plus some for dusting
- 1 tsp dried yeast
- ¼ tsp salt
- 80 ml (⅓ cup) water
- 1 tsp olive oil

PARENT PREP

- Preheat oven to 240°C/475°F/Gas 9
- Lay out: ingredients, mixing bowl, mixing spoon, board, table knife and rolling pin

ALL TOGETHER NOW!

❶ Put the flour, yeast, salt, water and oil into the bowl and mix.

❷ ✋ Use hands to combine the mixture into a ball of dough.

❸ Put the ball onto the board and squish, squash, pummel and play with it until it is soft and smooth. Leave the dough for at least 10 minutes (return it to the bowl and cover with a tea towel).

❹ Cut the dough into quarters.

❺ Dust a little flour onto the board and roll each pitta flat with rolling pin.

AND FINALLY…

Put each pitta directly on the oven rack and bake for 2 minutes. Use tongs to turn them over and cook for 1–2 minutes more. If you are not eating straight away, put them in a sealed freezer bag to keep soft.

MAKES
4

ACTIVITY
20

OVEN
4

Your child's schemas
(see pages 26–29)
- Transforming
- Rotating

Main tasks & skills
- Mixing
- Squishing
- Cutting
- Rolling

Allergy information

Egg	Not applicable
Dairy	Not applicable
Gluten	Avoid
Nut	Check labels for potential contamination

Family supper

There's something special about sitting down as a family to enjoy eating a home-cooked meal together at the end of the day – and even more so when the youngest member has done the cooking.

Mains

Puddings

Baked fish parcels

I've given a set of ingredients for this dish, but I often lay out a selection of veg and let the children choose what they want in their own parcel.

SERVES

4

ACTIVITY

15

OVEN

20

Your child's schemas
(see pages 26–29)
- Connecting
- Containing
- Enveloping
- Trajectory
- Transporting

Main tasks & skills
- Chopping
- Constructing
- Pouring
- Wrapping

Allergy information

Egg	Not applicable
Dairy	Not applicable
Gluten	Not applicable
Nut	Check labels for potential contamination

WHAT YOU NEED

- 4 fish fillets
- 8 cherry tomatoes
- 4 garlic cloves
- 4 handfuls spinach leaves
- 4 tbsp olive oil
- 4 large basil leaves

PARENT PREP

- Preheat oven to 180°C/350°F/Gas 4
- Lay out: ingredients, chopping board, table knife or child-safe knife, baking tray and 4 sheets of kitchen foil

ALL TOGETHER NOW!

❶ Put 1 fish fillet onto the middle of each sheet of foil.

❷ Put 1 handful of spinach and 1 large basil leaf torn into pieces on each piece of fish.

❸ Use the table knife to cut the tomatoes in half and put 4 halves on each fish.

❹ Use the table knife to cut the garlic in half and put 2 halves on each fish.

❺ Lift the sides of the foil and crumple it together at each end to make a 'boat'. Pour 1 tbsp olive oil into each.

❻ Roll the foil over at the top to seal it. Put the parcels onto the baking tray.

AND FINALLY…

Bake for 20 minutes for an average-sized fillet of salmon or cod (cook 5 minutes less if the fillets are small, or a more delicate fish, and longer if the fillets are large).

Salmon & tomato cannelloni

Children can use teaspoons to stuff the cannelloni, but the best way is with fingers – a good one for those who like to get messy.

WHAT YOU NEED

+ 120 g (⅔ cup) frozen, chopped spinach
+ 6 tbsp ricotta or cream cheese
+ 170 g boneless salmon (fresh or tinned)
+ 10 cannelloni tubes
+ 240 ml (1 cup) passata or ready-made tomato pasta sauce
+ 120 ml (½ cup) single cream

PARENT PREP

+ Preheat oven to 190°C/375°F/Gas 5
+ Leave the spinach out for at least an hour to defrost
+ Open and drain the salmon (tinned). Chop into small pieces (fresh)
+ Lay out: ingredients, mixing bowl, mixing spoon, oven-proof dish and kitchen foil

ALL TOGETHER NOW!

❶ Put the spinach, ricotta and salmon into the bowl and mix.

❷ Use fingers to stuff the salmon mix into the cannelloni tubes.

❸ Put the filled tubes into the dish.

❹ Put the passata and cream into a bowl and mix.

❺ Pour the passata sauce onto the tubes.

❻ Cover the dish with foil.

AND FINALLY...

Bake for 15 minutes before removing the foil, then for a further 15 minutes.

SERVES
3–4

ACTIVITY
20

OVEN
30

Your child's schemas
(see pages 26–29)
- Rotating
- Containing
- Enveloping
- Transforming
- Trajectory

Main tasks & skills
- Mixing
- Stuffing
- Pouring
- Covering

Allergy information

Egg	Check cannelloni label
Dairy	Substitute ricotta with extra spinach; use dairy-free cream
Gluten	Roll up gluten-free lasagne
Nut	Check labels for potential contamination

Sardine & vegetable COUSCOUS

I love sardines, not least for boosting that all-important oily-fish intake, but you can leave them out if you want a simple veggie couscous.

SERVES **3–4**

ACTIVITY **20**

Your child's schemas
(see pages 26–29)
• Connecting • Rotating
• Transporting

Main tasks & skills
• Mashing • Constructing
• Mixing

Allergy information

Egg	Not applicable
Dairy	Not applicable
Gluten	Use quinoa or rice instead of couscous
Nut	Check labels for potential contamination

WHAT YOU NEED

+ 150 g (¾ cup) couscous
+ 95 g tinned boneless sardines in olive oil
+ 5 tbsp tinned sweetcorn
+ 1–2 roasted red peppers (buy in a jar)
+ 50 g (⅓ cup) sultanas (or raisins)
+ 50 g (about 14) green beans

PARENT PREP

+ Put couscous in a heat-proof bowl and pour on just-boiled water to cover it. Set aside for 6 minutes
+ Cook green beans in boiling water for 10 minutes or use leftovers. Or have them raw
+ Open sardines, but do not drain off the oil
+ Lay out: ingredients and a fork

ALL TOGETHER NOW!

❶ Mash and mix the couscous with a fork to break it up.

❷ Tip the sardines and their oil onto the couscous and mix together.

❸ Snap the beans, using fingers, into little pieces and add to the bowl.

❹ Tear the red pepper into pieces and add.

❺ Add the sweetcorn and sultanas. Give the whole thing a good mix.

AND FINALLY...

Put on the table!

NB If you don't want to use sardines replace with 1 tbsp of olive oil and a squeeze of lemon.

Sausage pasta bake

This is a useful recipe if, like me, you often misjudge how much pasta to cook and end up with lots left over. Use any combination of cooked meat and vegetables.

WHAT YOU NEED

+ 450 g (4 cups) cooked fusilli or penne pasta (225 g/3 cups dried pasta, cooked)
+ 3 cooked sausages
+ 1 roasted pepper (buy in a jar)
+ 250 g (1 cup) ready-made tomato pasta sauce
+ 150 g (1½ cups) cheddar cheese

PARENT PREP

+ Grate the cheddar cheese or use a handled grater if you want the children to help
+ Preheat the oven to 210°C/410°F/Gas 7
+ Lay out: ingredients, oven-proof dish, 2 tablespoons, mixing bowl, table knife and chopping board

ALL TOGETHER NOW!

❶ Tear up the pepper and put into the mixing bowl.

❷ Use the table knife to chop the sausages into chunks and add to the bowl.

❸ Add the pasta.

❹ Spoon in the pasta sauce and mix well.

❺ Spoon the mixture into the oven-proof dish.

❻ Sprinkle over the grated cheese.

AND FINALLY...

Bake in the oven for 15–20 minutes until the cheese is melted and sizzling.

NB If you want to keep cooked pasta overnight to use in this recipe, cool in running water, cover and put in the fridge as soon as possible after cooking to prevent the growth of harmful bacteria.

SERVES
3–4

ACTIVITY
20

OVEN
20

Your child's schemas
(see pages 26–29)
• Transporting   • Transforming
• Connecting   • Enveloping

Main tasks & skills
• Chopping   • Spooning
• Mixing   • Sprinkling

Allergy information

Egg	Check pasta label
Dairy	Leave out cheese
Gluten	Use gluten-free pasta
Nut	Check labels for potential contamination

Vegetable tart art

Get them to create a fun, framed picture and then bake it! Like pizza, there are lots of possible toppings you could have. I like to lay out the options and let them choose.

SERVES
2–4

ACTIVITY
20

OVEN
30

Your child's schemas
(see pages 26–29)
• Connecting
• Transporting

Main tasks & skills
• Mixing
• Constructing
• Painting

Allergy information

Egg	Check pastry label
Dairy	Check pastry label and leave out mozzarella
Gluten	Use gluten-free puff pastry
Nut	Check labels for potential contamination

WHAT YOU NEED

✦ 1 sheet (approx 220 g) ready-rolled puff pastry
✦ 4 tbsp ready-made tomato pasta sauce
✦ 4 tbsp chopped frozen spinach
✦ 2 roasted red peppers in oil (buy in a jar)
✦ 200 g fresh mozzarella
✦ 4 large basil leaves (optional)

PARENT PREP

✦ Preheat oven to 190°C/375°F/Gas 5
✦ Leave the spinach out for at least an hour – to start to defrost
✦ Lay out: ingredients, baking tray, table knife, mixing bowl, mixing spoon and pastry brush

ALL TOGETHER NOW!

❶ Put the pastry sheet on the tray and use a table knife to lightly 'draw' a 2-cm 'frame' around the edge.

❷ Put the tomato sauce and the spinach in the bowl and mix.

❸ Spoon on the spinach-tomato mix and spread around, trying not to get any on the 'frame'.

❹ Tear the peppers, mozzarella and basil into pieces and arrange them on the tart to make a 'picture'.

❺ Use the pastry brush to brush the oil from the pepper jar around the 'frame'.

AND FINALLY…

Bake in the oven for 30 minutes.

Salmon fishcakes

An easy, tasty fishcake recipe, which is another family favourite. If children are not keen on squishing fresh fish, use tinned, boneless salmon and mush with a fork.

WHAT YOU NEED
+ 340 g boneless/skinless salmon
+ 2 spring onions
+ 50 g (1 cup) breadcrumbs
+ 1 tbsp sweet chilli sauce
+ 1 tbsp parsley
+ 2 tbsp plain flour

PARENT PREP
+ Chop parsley
+ Lay out: ingredients, mixing bowl, mixing spoon, child-safe scissors, plate or chopping board

ALL TOGETHER NOW!

❶ Put the salmon into the mixing bowl and squish with hands until it is mushed up.

❷ Cut the spring onions into little pieces with child-safe scissors and put into the bowl.

❸ Add breadcrumbs, sweet chilli sauce and parsley. Mix together.

❹ Use hands to shape 8 small fishcakes and place on a plate or board.

❺ Sprinkle the flour over both sides.

AND FINALLY…

Chill the fishcakes in the fridge for a minimum of 20 minutes to stop them breaking up on cooking. Fry gently in oil, for about 3 minutes on each side.

SERVES
2–4

ACTIVITY
25

CHILL
20

Your child's schemas
(see pages 26–29)
• Enveloping   • Transporting

Main tasks & skills
• Squishing   • Sculpting
• Cutting   • Sprinkling
• Mixing

Allergy information

Egg	Not applicable
Dairy	Not applicable
Gluten	Use gluten-free breadcrumbs
Nut	Check labels for potential contamination

Stuffed pepper boats

My two enjoy pretending to be sharks – taking big bites out of these yummy little boats. For more fun use potato skins to make crisps using the chip recipe on page 55.

SERVES

4

ACTIVITY

25

OVEN

25

Your child's schemas
(see pages 26–29)
• Containing
• Transporting

Main tasks & skills
• Cleaning   • Mixing
• Mashing   • Stuffing

Allergy information

Egg	Not applicable
Dairy	Substitute cheese and cream for 2 tbsp of dairy-free spread
Gluten	Not applicable
Nut	Check labels for potential contamination

WHAT YOU NEED
✦ 2 large baking potatoes
✦ 3 tbsp sour cream
✦ 70 g (⅔ cup) cheddar cheese
✦ 1 tsp parsley
✦ 3 peppers
✦ Small pinch paprika

PARENT PREP
✦ Bake potatoes for 1 hour at 200°C/390°F/Gas 6. Halve and leave to cool
✦ Reheat oven to 200°C/390°F/Gas 6
✦ Chop parsley, or snip with child-safe scissors
✦ Cut peppers in half lengthways; or they can try with a table knife
✦ Lay out: ingredients, mixing bowl, potato masher, tablespoon, fork, baking tray and bowl of water

ALL TOGETHER NOW!

❶ Pull the seeds and white bits out of the pepper halves.

❷ Wash the peppers in a bowl of water, making sure that all the seeds are removed. Put on a baking tray.

❸ Scoop out the flesh from the potato and mash in a bowl.

❹ Add the sour cream, cheese and parsley to the bowl and mix.

❺ Stuff the potato mix into each pepper half.

❻ Sprinkle a little paprika over the tops.

AND FINALLY...

Bake for 25 minutes. Make sails using toothpicks and sliced ham/lettuce/herbs (optional). You can also wrap them in foil and cook in barbecue/campfire coals.

Vegetable korma

It's never too soon to introduce young children to different flavours such as mild curries; it can help them be more adventurous in trying new tastes later in life.

WHAT YOU NEED

- 400 ml coconut milk
- 2 tbsp korma paste
- 400 g (4 medium) potatoes (or 200 g potatoes and 200 g sweet potato)
- 150 g (1 cup) frozen peas
- 1 large (or 2 small) courgettes
- 1½ tbsp black onion (nigella) seeds
- Handful fresh coriander (optional)

PARENT PREP

- Preheat oven to 180°C/350°F/Gas 4
- Peel and boil potatoes until cooked or use leftovers
- Lay out: ingredients, mixing bowl, fork, table knife, chopping board and oven-proof dish

ALL TOGETHER NOW!

❶ Pour the coconut milk into the bowl.

❷ Add the korma paste and mix with a fork.

❸ Use the table knife to cut the potatoes and courgette into bite-sized chunks and put into the bowl.

❹ Add the peas and black onion seeds. Mix.

❺ Pour into the oven-proof dish.

❻ If you are using it, tear the coriander leaves and sprinkle them on the top.

AND FINALLY…

Season and bake for 25 minutes. Serve with rice and/or naan bread (see recipe on page 98) to soak up the curry sauce.

SERVES 2–4

ACTIVITY 25   **OVEN** 25

Your child's schemas
(see pages 26–29)
- Trajectory
- Transporting
- Transforming

Main tasks & skills
- Pouring
- Chopping
- Mixing
- Tearing

Allergy information

Egg	Not applicable
Dairy	Not applicable
Gluten	Not applicable
Nut	Use tikka paste and check label. Check with allergist about reaction to coconut

Naan bread

This is one of the easiest and quickest breads to make, so it's ideal for cooking with a toddler as well as being the perfect curry accompaniment.

MAKES
4

ACTIVITY
20

GRILL
4

Your child's schemas
(see pages 26–29)
• Transforming

Main tasks & skills
• Mixing • Cutting
• Squishing • Rolling

Allergy information

Egg	Not applicable
Dairy	Use dairy-free yoghurt
Gluten	Avoid
Nut	Check labels for potential contamination

WHAT YOU NEED

+ 250 g (2 cups) plain flour, plus a little for dusting
+ ¼ tsp salt
+ ½ tsp bicarbonate of soda
+ 180 g (⅔ cup) Greek-style yoghurt
+ ½ tsp oil

PARENT PREP

+ Lay out: ingredients, mixing bowl, mixing spoon, board, table knife, baking tray, pastry brush or kitchen roll and rolling pin (optional)

VARIATION

Add toppings or seeds if you want to flavour

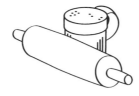

ALL TOGETHER NOW!

❶ Put the flour, salt, bicarbonate of soda and yoghurt into the bowl and mix.

❷ ✋ Squish the mixture with hands until you have a ball of dough.

❸ Dust a little flour onto the board and squish, squash, pummel and play around with the dough until it is soft.

❹ Use the table knife to cut the dough into quarters.

❺ Use hands (or rolling pin) to squash each ball into a rough, flat oval.

❻ Brush or rub the oil over the baking tray. Put the bread on the tray.

AND FINALLY...

Put the tray under a hot grill for 1–2 minutes each side, until the naans are light brown and puffy.

Chicken & ham pie

I love this recipe for using up leftover chicken and ham. If your child is too young to use a rolling pin, use ready-rolled puff pastry.

WHAT YOU NEED

- 200 g (1½ cups) cooked chicken
- 150 g (1 cup) cooked ham
- 100 g (1 cup) mushrooms
- 200 ml (¾ cup) tinned cream of chicken soup
- 1 tbsp parsley
- 230 g puff pastry
- Flour for dusting
- 1 egg

PARENT PREP

- Finely chop parsley, or use a handled herb chopper so your children can help
- Preheat oven to 210°C/410°F/Gas 7
- Lay out: ingredients, 1-litre pie dish, mixing bowl, mixing spoon, tablespoon, teaspoon, fork, rolling pin, chopping board, pastry brush, cookie cutters in fun shapes (optional) and small bowl

ALL TOGETHER NOW!

❶ Tear the chicken, ham and mushrooms into bite-sized pieces and put them into a large bowl.

❷ Pour in the soup and parsley. Mix, then spoon into the pie dish and set aside.

❸ Dust the flour on the chopping board and rolling pin. Roll the pastry into a rough circle, big enough to cover the pie dish.

❹ Place the pastry over the chicken mixture. Press gently around the edge.

❺ Pull off excess pastry and use it to mould fun shapes with hands or cookie cutters. Decorate the pie with them.

❻ Whisk the egg with a fork in the small bowl. Brush the egg over the pie with a pastry brush.

AND FINALLY...

Bake for 25 minutes until golden brown.

SERVES

4

ACTIVITY

25

OVEN

25

Your child's schemas
(see pages 26–29)
- Rotating
- Enveloping
- Containing
- Transporting

Main tasks & skills
- Tearing
- Mixing
- Rolling
- Painting

Allergy information

Egg	Check puff pastry label and brush top with milk
Dairy	Avoid
Gluten	Use gluten-free puff pastry
Nut	Check labels for potential contamination

Pea & ham quiche 1: shortcrust pastry

This is a fun, easy pastry and can be used to make all sorts of things. I have split the recipe into two parts (see opposite).

MAKES

220 g

ACTIVITY 30

OVEN 15

Your child's schemas
(see pages 26–29)
- Enveloping
- Transforming

Main tasks & skills
- Tickling
- Rolling
- Squishing
- Pricking

Allergy information

Egg	Not applicable
Dairy	Use dairy-free spread
Gluten	Use gluten-free flour
Nut	Check labels for potential contamination

WHAT YOU NEED
- 140 g (1 cup) plain flour plus some for dusting
- Small pinch of salt
- 65 g unsalted butter
- 35 ml water

PARENT PREP
- Preheat oven to 200°C/390°F/Gas 6
- Lay out: ingredients, mixing bowl, board or mat for rolling on, rolling pin, kitchen foil, 18-cm flan tin, table knife, chopping board and fork

TIP
This is easier to make in two sessions. When they've made the pastry, instead of baking it, wrap it in cling film and put in the fridge (up to 2 days). Or freeze it. Don't forget to blind-bake it in time to do the filling!

ALL TOGETHER NOW!

❶ Cut the butter into little pieces using a table knife.

❷ Put the flour, salt and butter pieces into the bowl. Rub butter into the flour using fingertips, until it looks like breadcrumbs.

❸ Sprinkle over water and squish with hands to make a pastry ball.

❹ Dust flour on the board and rolling pin to prevent sticking. Roll the pastry into a rough circle about 3 mm thick.

❺ Lay the pastry over the flan tin. Lightly press into the sides, leaving the pastry to overlap over the top. Do not trim excess.

❻ Use the fork to prick holes in the base. Loosely crumple 4 pieces of foil into large balls and put on the base.

AND FINALLY...

Bake for 15 minutes. Set aside for filling.

Pea & ham quiche 2: the filling

This part of a quiche is do-able by most toddlers. So if they are not yet ready to make pastry, do part 1 yourself, or use ready-made shortcrust.

WHAT YOU NEED

- 18-cm blind-baked shortcrust pastry base (see part 1, facing page)
- 3 eggs
- 120 ml (½ cup) single cream
- 120 g (¾ cup) frozen peas
- 60 g (⅔ cup) grated cheddar cheese
- 60 g (½ cup) ham

PARENT PREP

- Preheat oven to 190°C/375°F/Gas 5
- Grate cheddar cheese
- Lay out: ingredients, large mixing bowl and fork

TIP

Most quiche fillings can be assembled by a toddler, so check out your adult recipe books for ideas

ALL TOGETHER NOW!

❶ Break the eggs into the large bowl. Whisk with a fork.

❷ Tear the ham into small pieces and add to the bowl.

❸ Add the cream, peas and cheese. Mix well with a fork.

❹ Pour the mixture into the pastry base.

AND FINALLY...

Season and bake in the oven for 40–45 minutes until set. Run a sharp knife around the top of the flan tin to remove excess pastry.

SERVES
4

ACTIVITY
15

OVEN
45

Your child's schemas
(see pages 26–29)
- Trajectory
- Containing
- Rotating

Main tasks & skills
- Whisking
- Pouring
- Tearing

Allergy information

Egg	Avoid
Dairy	Use dairy-free cream and leave out cheese
Gluten	Use gluten-free shortcrust pastry
Nut	Check labels for potential contamination

Frozen yoghurt lollies

These easy tasty lollies are great for using up fruit that has gone squishy. You can make all sorts of colour and flavour combinations using different fruits and flavoured yoghurts.

MAKES

6

ACTIVITY

20

FREEZE

120

Your child's schemas
(see pages 26–29)
• Transforming
• Containing

Main tasks & skills
• Mashing   • Spooning
• Mixing

Allergy information

Egg	Not applicable
Dairy	Use dairy-free yoghurt and cream
Gluten	Not applicable
Nut	Check labels for potential contamination

WHAT YOU NEED
◆ 6 raspberries
◆ 125 g (½ cup) Greek-style or natural yoghurt
◆ 125 g (½ cup) raspberry or strawberry yoghurt
◆ ½ tsp vanilla extract
◆ 50 ml (4 tbsp) cream

PARENT PREP
◆ Lay out: ingredients, 6 ice-lolly moulds, mixing bowl, mixing spoon, potato masher (or fork) and 2 tablespoons

ALL TOGETHER NOW!

❶ Mash the raspberries into the bowl with a masher or fork.

❷ Add the Greek-style yoghurt, flavoured yoghurt, vanilla extract and cream. Mix.

❸ Spoon and scrape the mixture into ice-lolly moulds.

AND FINALLY…

Freeze for a minimum of 2 hours.

Fruit fool

My mum used to make fool nearly every week, using fruit that was in season: plums, gooseberries and blackcurrants. We loved all the different colours.

WHAT YOU NEED

+ 400 g fruit, e.g. plums, gooseberries, blackcurrants or mixed berries
+ 125 g (½ cup) Greek-style or natural yoghurt
+ 125 g (½ cup) ready-made custard

PARENT PREP

+ Gently boil fruit in about 4 tbsp water until mushy. Leave to cool
+ Lay out: ingredients, sieve, tablespoon, mixing spoon and mixing bowl

ALL TOGETHER NOW!

❶ Put the sieve over the bowl. Tip the cooked fruit into the sieve.

❷ Use the back of the tablespoon to squash the fruit in the sieve. If you are using fruit that has stones, pick them out.

❸ Once all the fruit flesh is through the sieve, scrape the mush off the bottom of the sieve into the bowl.

❹ Dollop on the yoghurt and mix.

❺ Dollop on the custard and mix.

AND FINALLY...

Cover and put in the fridge for a minimum of 1 hour. Serve as it is or with cream.

SERVES
2–4

ACTIVITY
20

CHILL
60

Your child's schemas
(see pages 26–29)
• Transforming
• Rotating

Main tasks & skills
• Squashing   • Mixing
• Spooning

Allergy information

Egg	Check custard label
Dairy	Use dairy-free custard and yoghurt
Gluten	Not applicable
Nut	Check labels for potential contamination

Fruit salad rainbow

cone
A quick and easy snack or pudding, which is also fun to make with a group of children as a pre-school or party activity.

MAKES

4

ACTIVITY

20

Your child's schemas
(see pages 26–29)
• Connecting
• Containing
• Transporting

Main tasks & skills
• Counting
• Constructing
• Chopping
• Decorating

Allergy information

Egg	Not applicable
Dairy	Use dairy-free cream and plastic cup instead of a cone
Gluten	Use gluten-free ice-cream cones
Nut	Check labels for potential contamination

WHAT YOU NEED
+ 4 flat-bottomed ice-cream cones
+ 8 blueberries
+ 4 green grapes
+ 1 banana
+ 1 easy-peeler orange
+ 4 strawberries
+ Squirty cream and sprinkles to decorate

PARENT PREP
+ Hull the strawberries
+ Lay out: ingredients, chopping board and table (or child-safe) knife

ALL TOGETHER NOW!

❶ Put 2 blueberries into each cone.

❷ Use the table knife to cut the grapes in half. Put 2 halves into each cone.

❸ Use the table knife to slice the banana. Put an equal amount into each cone.

❹ Peel the orange and put 2 slices into each cone.

❺ Use the table knife to cut the strawberries into quarters. Put them into each cone.

❻ Squirt on the cream and decorate with sprinkles.

AND FINALLY…

Serve with a teaspoon.

Fruity yoghurt pots

This is a quick snack/pudding to make just before eating. If you want to make the pots in advance, keep the crushed digestives to one side and sprinkle on just beforehand.

WHAT YOU NEED
+ 1 banana
+ 30 blueberries
+ 3 digestive biscuits
+ 250 g (1 cup/240 ml) natural or Greek-style yoghurt

PARENT PREP
+ Lay out: ingredients, 4 small plastic cups, 2 tablespoons, mixing bowl, small mixing bowl, table knife and chopping board

ALL TOGETHER NOW!

❶ Cut the banana into slices with a table knife. Put it into the mixing bowl.

❷ Add the blueberries to the bowl.

❸ Add the yogurt to the bowl and mix.

❹ Divide the mixture into plastic cups.

❺ Crush the digestives between fingers over a small bowl until they are in little pieces/ big crumbs.

❻ Sprinkle the digestive crumbs onto the top of each cup.

AND FINALLY…

Serve with a teaspoon.

MAKES
4

ACTIVITY
15

Your child's schemas
(see pages 26–29)
• Containing
• Enveloping
• Rotating

Main tasks & skills
• Chopping
• Mixing
• Counting
• Crushing

Allergy information

Egg	Not applicable
Dairy	Check digestive label and use dairy-free yoghurt
Gluten	Use gluten-free biscuits
Nut	Check labels for potential contamination

Apple cake

An upside-down cake that you can make with any fruit/s you like. It is best eaten warm with cream, custard or ice cream, but it is also delicious to have cold.

SERVES
6

ACTIVITY **25** OVEN **30**

Your child's schemas
(see pages 26–29)
• Enveloping
• Connecting
• Rotating

Main tasks & skills
• Rubbing
• Constructing
• Mixing
• Spooning

Allergy information

Egg	Avoid
Dairy	Use dairy-free spread
Gluten	Use gluten-free flour
Nut	Check labels for potential contamination

WHAT YOU NEED
✦ 2 dessert apples
✦ ½ tsp of butter for greasing
✦ 125 g butter
✦ 125 g (⅔ cup) sugar
✦ 125 g (1 cup) self-raising flour
✦ 2 eggs

PARENT PREP
✦ Peel, core and cut apples into slices. If not using immediately, squeeze over a little lemon juice to stop them going brown.
✦ Take butter out of fridge at least an hour before using, to soften
✦ Preheat oven to 180°C/350°F/Gas 4
✦ Lay out: ingredients, 18-cm cake tin, mixing bowl, mixing spoon and 2 tablespoons.

ALL TOGETHER NOW!

❶ Rub half a teaspoon of the butter all over the cake tin.

❷ Lay the apple slices out on the bottom of the tin. Set aside.

❸ Put the butter and sugar in the mixing bowl and squish and stir with a mixing spoon until they are combined.

❹ Add the eggs to the bowl and mix.

❺ Add the flour to the bowl and do a final mix until the flour has been mixed in.

❻ Use 2 spoons to spoon and scrape the mixture onto the apples and spread out with the back of a spoon.

AND FINALLY…

Bake in the oven for 30 minutes until golden brown and springy to the touch. Turn out onto a plate with the apples on top

Croissant pudding

Possibly the easiest bread-and-butter pudding ever. I've used strawberries, but you could make it with any fruit – fresh or tinned.

WHAT YOU NEED
- ◆ 2 croissants
- ◆ 4 large strawberries
- ◆ 1 egg
- ◆ 250 ml (1 cup) milk

PARENT PREP
- ◆ Preheat oven to 190°C/375°F/Gas 5
- ◆ Hull strawberries
- ◆ Lay out: ingredients, bowl, fork, table knife, chopping board and oven-proof dish

VARIATIONS
If you don't have croissants, spread butter on 3 slices of bread and tear them up. The pudding is also yummy made with brioche

ALL TOGETHER NOW!

❶ Tear the croissants into pieces. Put them into the dish.

❷ Use a table knife to cut the strawberries into quarters. Add to the dish.

❸ Break an egg into the bowl.

❹ Add the milk and whisk with a fork.

❺ Pour the milk mix onto the croissants and strawberries.

❻ Press the croissant bits down with the fork to soak.

AND FINALLY…

Bake in the oven for 30–35 minutes until the pudding is set.

SERVES
3–4

ACTIVITY
20

OVEN
35

Your child's schemas
(see pages 26–29)
- Transporting
- Trajectory
- Rotating

Main tasks & skills
- Tearing
- Whisking
- Cutting
- Pouring

Allergy information

Egg	Avoid
Dairy	Use dairy-free milk and spread bread with dairy-free spread
Gluten	Use gluten-free bread or croissants
Nut	Check labels for potential contamination

Fruity mess

This is a version of Eton Mess and you can make it with any fruit combinations you like. Swapping the banana for 60 g of blueberries works well.

SERVES

4

ACTIVITY

25

Your child's schemas
(see pages 26–29)
• Containing
• Transforming

Main tasks & skills
• Mashing   • Chopping
• Mixing   • Spooning

Allergy information

Egg	Avoid
Dairy	Use dairy-free cream and yoghurt
Gluten	Not applicable
Nut	Check labels for potential contamination

WHAT YOU NEED

✦ 150 g (¾ cup) strawberries
✦ 100 ml (½ cup) double or whipping cream
✦ 100 g (½ cup) Greek-style yoghurt
✦ 4 meringues (or 1 large pavlova base)
✦ 1 banana

PARENT PREP

✦ Hull and quarter strawberries. Set aside one-third for decorating
✦ Whip cream into soft peaks or use ready-whipped
✦ Lay out: ingredients, 4 plastic glasses, large mixing bowl, potato masher or fork, 2 tablespoons, table knife and chopping board

ALL TOGETHER NOW!

❶ Put two-thirds of the strawberries in the bowl and squash them with a masher or fork until they are mushy.

❷ Spoon the whipped cream and yoghurt into the bowl and mix.

❸ Use the table knife to chop the banana into slices and add to the bowl.

❹ Break the meringues into small pieces and put them in the bowl. Mix again.

❺ Use 2 tablespoons to spoon and scrape the mixture into plastic glasses

❻ Decorate with the remaining quartered strawberries.

AND FINALLY...

Serve with a teaspoon.

Raspberry cheesecake

My mum used to make this cheesecake for us and I love seeing my children enjoy it too – both the making and the eating. You can use different yoghurts to vary the flavour.

WHAT YOU NEED

- 100 g (about 7) digestive biscuits
- 50 g (4 tbsp) butter
- 75 g (⅓ cup) cream cheese
- 50 g (3 tbsp) sugar
- 140 ml (⅔ cup) double cream
- 125 g (½ cup) raspberry yoghurt
- Raspberries to decorate (optional)

PARENT PREP

- Put digestive biscuits into a plastic freezer bag
- Gently melt butter and transfer to a jug
- Whip 140 ml cream or use ready whipped
- Lay out: 18-cm round flan or cake tin or 4 ramekins, rolling pin, 2 mixing bowls, 2 tablespoons and 2 mixing spoons

ALL TOGETHER NOW!

❶ Hold the end of the freezer bag while they bash it with a rolling pin – until the digestives look like breadcrumbs.

❷ Put crushed biscuits into a bowl. Pour on melted butter and mix.

❸ Put the crumbs into the cake tin/ ramekins and press down with hands.
Put it into the fridge.

❹ Put the cream cheese and sugar into the other bowl. Mix well.

❺ Add the whipped cream and yoghurt. Fold together with a tablespoon until just combined.

❻ Spoon the mixture onto the biscuit base and spread out.

AND FINALLY...

Chill for at least 2 hours and decorate with raspberries to serve.

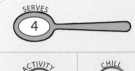

SERVES
4

ACTIVITY
25

CHILL
120

Your child's schemas
(see pages 26–29)
- Transforming
- Trajectory
- Enveloping

Main tasks & skills
- Bashing
- Spooning
- Squashing
- Spreading
- Mixing

Allergy information

Egg	Not applicable
Dairy	Avoid
Gluten	Use gluten-free digestives
Nut	Check labels for potential contamination

Apple & blackberry crumble

This is my eldest daughter's favourite pudding. The first time she tickled the butter into the flour, aged two, was the origin of 'tickle fingers'!

SERVES

4

ACTIVITY 30

OVEN 30

Your child's schemas
(see pages 26–29)
- Enveloping
- Connecting

Main tasks & skills
- Constructing
- Tickling
- Burying

Allergy information

Egg	Not applicable
Dairy	Use dairy-free spread
Gluten	Use gluten-free flour
Nut	Check labels for potential contamination

WHAT YOU NEED

- 3 dessert apples
- 10 blackberries
- 55 g butter
- 130 g (1 cup) plain flour
- 2 tbsp sugar
- ⅛ tsp ground cinnamon (optional)

PARENT PREP

- Peel, core and cut dessert apples into slices. I use an 'apple master' so they can help by turning the handle. If not using the apples immediately, squeeze a little lemon juice over them to stop them going brown
- Preheat oven to 220°C/425°F/Gas 7
- Lay out: ingredients, oven-proof dish, mixing bowl, mixing spoon, table knife and chopping board

ALL TOGETHER NOW!

❶ Lay out the apple slices in an oven-proof dish.

❷ Add the blackberries, spacing them out. Set aside.

❸ Cut the butter into little pieces with a table knife.

❹ Put the flour and butter pieces into the bowl. Rub the butter into the flour, using fingertips, until it looks like breadcrumbs.

❺ Add the sugar and, if using, cinnamon. Mix together.

❻ Spoon the crumble mixture on the apples and blackberries, spreading it out evenly.

AND FINALLY...

Bake in the oven for 30 minutes until light brown. Serve warm or cold with cream, ice cream or custard.

Useful bits & pieces

Here are some handy, easy-to-use charts that you may find useful, especially if your child shows an interest in measuring, has an allergy, or you want to find a recipe to match leftovers/perishable food in your fridge.

Measuring cups & spoons
Familiar to anyone who uses American recipes, measuring in cups and spoons (1 cup, ½ cup, ⅓ cup, ¼ cup, 1 tbsp, ½ tbsp, 1 tsp, ½ tsp) is a great way for a young child to start to learn to do their own measuring.

Filling the right cup or spoon to the top, the right number of times is easier for a young child than learning to operate and read measuring scales. However, if you've never used this system, there are a couple of things to bear in mind:

1 Because you are measuring in volume not weight, conversion from grams is not precise, particularly if the ingredient you are measuring is light, chunky or variable in size.

2 To help ensure you get as close as possible to the right measurement, over-fill the cup or spoon and then level off the top with a hand or table knife.

Conversion chart

	1 cup	1 tbsp
Plain flour	125–140 g	7–8 g
Self-raising flour	125–140 g	7–8 g
Caster sugar	200–215 g	12–14 g
Light-brown sugar	165–180 g	10–12 g
Demerara sugar	185–200 g	12 g
Cocoa powder	90–100 g	6–8 g
Chocolate chips	170–180 g	12–14 g
Long-grain rice (uncooked)	185–200 g	
Long-grain rice (cooked)	125 g	
Oats	100 g	6 g
Cheddar cheese (coarsely grated)	90–100 g	5 g
Parmesan cheese (finely grated)	75–90 g	5 g
Breadcrumbs (fresh)	50–60 g	
Sweetcorn (tinned)	250 g	
Peas	150 g	
Yoghurt	250 g	14–16 g
Blueberries	100 g	
Raisins	120–135 g	
Currants	150 g	
Couscous (uncooked)	180 g	
Mushrooms (sliced)	75–100 g	

Liquids
240 ml = 1 cup
120 ml = ½ cup

80 ml = ⅓ cup
60 ml = ¼ cup
15 ml = 1 tbsp

Dried yeast
7 g = 2 tsp

Allergy chart

If you need to consider an allergy (egg, dairy, gluten or nut), this chart shows which recipes you can do using a traffic-light system. Green means 'go for it', yellow 'okay with substitutions' and red 'avoid altogether'.

Recipes	Egg	Dairy	Gluten	Nut
Blueberry yoghurt muffins – page 46	🟡	🟡	🟡	🟢
Overnight oats – page 47	🟢	🟡	🟡	🟢
Baked eggs Benedict – page 48	🔴	🟡	🟡	🟢
Baked pancake – page 49	🔴	🟡	🟡	🟢
Bacon & egg soda bread – page 50	🟡	🟡	🟡	🟢
Kedgeree – page 51	🟡	🟡	🟡	🟡
Nachos – page 54	🟢	🟡	🟡	🟢
Pitta chips – page 55	🟢	🟢	🟡	🟢
Tzatziki – page 56	🟢	🟡	🟢	🟢
Egg-free arancini – page 57	🟢	🔴	🟡	🟢
Cheese straws – page 58	🟢	🟡	🟡	🟢
Courgette & carrot bites – page 59	🔴	🟡	🟡	🟢
Breadsticks – page 60	🟢	🟢	🟡	🟢
Cheesy biscuits – page 61	🟡	🔴	🟡	🟢
Guacamole – page 62	🟢	🟢	🟢	🟢

Recipes	Egg	Dairy	Gluten	Nut
Banana & cherry flapjacks – page 63	○	○	○	○
Chocolate biscuit cake – page 64	○	○	○	○
Egg-free cookies – page 65	○	○	○	○
Chocolate fork biscuits – page 66	○	○	○	○
Lemon yoghurt cake – page 67	○	○	○	○
Melting moments – page 68	○	○	○	○
Traditional shortbread – page 69	○	○	○	○
Banana & peanut butter cakes – page 70	●	○	○	○
Chocolate cake squares – page 71	○	○	○	○
Carrot cakes – page 72	○	○	○	○
Mini scones – page 73	○	○	○	○
Curried chicken wraps – page 76	○	○	○	○
Ham & mushroom pizza – page 77	○	●	○	○
Pirate treasure salad – page 78	○	○	○	○
Smoked mackerel pâté – page 79	○	●	○	○
Tuna mayo pitta pockets – page 80	○	○	○	○
Chicken bread baskets – page 81	○	○	○	○
Frittata – page 82	●	○	○	○
Tomato salsa bruschetta – page 83	○	○	○	○
Vegetable samosas – page 84	○	○	●	○
Cheese & bacon muffins – page 86	●	●	○	○
Homemade pitta bread – page 87	○	○	●	○
Baked fish parcels – page 90	○	○	○	○

Recipes	Egg	Dairy	Gluten	Nut
Salmon & tomato cannelloni – page 91	●	●	●	●
Sardine & vegetable couscous – page 92	●	●	●	●
Sausage pasta bake – page 93	●	●	●	●
Vegetable tart art – page 94	●	●	●	●
Salmon fishcakes – page 95	●	●	●	●
Stuffed pepper boats – page 96	●	●	●	●
Vegetable korma – page 97	●	●	●	●
Naan bread – page 98	●	●	●	●
Chicken & ham pie – page 99	●	●	●	●
Shortcrust pastry – page 100	●	●	●	●
Pea & ham quiche filling – page 101	●	●	●	●
Frozen yoghurt lollies – page 102	●	●	●	●
Fruit fool – page 103	●	●	●	●
Fruit salad rainbow cone – page 104	●	●	●	●
Fruity yoghurt pots – page 105	●	●	●	●
Apple cake – page 106	●	●	●	●
Croissant pudding – page 107	●	●	●	●
Fruity mess – page 108	●	●	●	●
Raspberry cheesecake – page 109	●	●	●	●
Apple & blackberry crumble – page 110	●	●	●	●
Sweet shortcrust pastry – page 112	●	●	●	●
Custard tart filling – page 113	●	●	●	●

Using up your leftovers

Never waste your leftovers! Use them to create a delicious dish or meal the following day. Search this chart for the perishable ingredient you want to use up and see which recipes you can use it in.

Apples
Apple & blackberry crumble
Apple cake

Avocado
Nachos
Guacamole

Bacon
Bacon & egg soda bread
Cheese & bacon muffins
Courgette & carrot bites

Banana
Banana & cherry flapjacks
Banana & peanut butter cakes
Fruit salad rainbow cone
Fruity mess
Fruity yoghurt pots

Basil
Baked fish parcels
Bruschetta
Ham & mushroom pizza

Vegetable tart art

Blackcurrants
Fruit fool

Blackberries
Apple & blackberry crumble

Blueberries
Blueberry yoghurt muffins
Fruit salad rainbow cone
Fruity yoghurt pots
Overnight oats
Pirate treasure salad

Bread/Breadcrumbs
Tomato salsa bruschetta
Chicken bread baskets
Croissant pudding
Egg-free arancini
Salmon fishcakes

Broccoli
Egg-free arancini
Frittata

Carrot
Carrot cakes
Courgette & carrot bites
Frittata
Pirate treasure salad
Vegetable samosas

Cheddar cheese
Cheese & bacon muffins
Cheese straws
Cheesy biscuits
Courgette & carrot bites
Egg-free arancini
Frittata
Nachos
Pea & ham quiche
Sausage pasta bake
Stuffed pepper boats
Tuna mayo pitta pockets

Chicken (cooked)
Chicken bread baskets
Chicken & ham pie
Curried chicken wraps

Coriander
Vegetable korma

Courgette
Courgette & carrot bites
Frittata
Vegetable korma

Cream (double)
Frozen yoghurt lollies
Fruit salad rainbow cone
Fruity mess
Raspberry cheesecake

Cream (single)
Frozen yoghurt lollies
Kedgeree
Pea & ham quiche
Salmon & tomato cannelloni
Smoked mackerel pâté

Cream (sour)
Stuffed pepper boats

Cream cheese
Carrot cakes
Egg-free arancini
Raspberry cheesecake
Salmon & tomato cannelloni
Smoked mackerel pâté

Custard
Apple & blackberry crumble
Apple cake
Custard tart
Fruit fool

Digestive biscuits
Chocolate biscuit cake
Fruity yoghurt pots
Raspberry cheesecake

Eggs
Apple cake
Bacon & egg soda bread
Baked eggs Benedict
Baked pancake
Banana & peanut butter
  cakes
Carrot cakes
Cheese & bacon muffins
Chicken & ham pie
Chocolate cake squares
Courgette & carrot bites
Croissant pudding
Custard tart
Frittata
Pea & ham quiche

English muffins
Baked eggs Benedict

Ham & mushroom pizza

Filo pastry
Vegetable samosas

Fish (fresh)
Baked fish parcels
Salmon & tomato cannelloni
Salmon fishcakes

Fruit
Apple cake
Apple & blackberry crumble
Raspberry cheesecake
Croissant pudding
Apple & blackberry crumble
Frozen yoghurt lollies
Fruit fool
Fruit salad rainbow cone

Garlic
Baked fish parcels
Guacamole

Gooseberries
Fruit fool

Grapes
Fruit salad rainbow cone
Pirate treasure salad

Green beans
Frittata
Sardine & vegetable
  couscous
Vegetable samosas

Ham
Baked eggs Benedict
Chicken & ham pie
Ham & mushroom pizza
Pea & ham quiche

Lemon
Lemon yoghurt cake
Smoked mackerel pâté
Tzatziki

Lettuce
Pirate treasure salad

Lime
Curried chicken wraps
Guacamole
Nachos
Tomato salsa bruschetta

Mackerel (smoked)
Kedgeree
Smoked mackerel pâté

Mayonnaise
Baked eggs Benedict
Chicken bread baskets
Curried chicken wraps
Tuna mayo pitta pockets

Mango chutney
Curried chicken wraps
Vegetable samosas

Milk
Bacon & egg soda bread
Baked pancake

Banana & peanut butter
  cakes
Breadsticks
Cheese & bacon muffins
Chocolate cake squares
Croissant pudding
Frittata

Mint
Tzatziki

Mozzarella
Ham & mushroom pizza
Pirate treasure salad
Vegetable tart art

Mushrooms
Chicken & ham pie
Ham & mushroom pizza

Onion
Frittata
Vegetable samosas

Orange
Carrot cakes
Fruit salad rainbow cone

Parsley
Chicken bread baskets
Chicken & ham pie
Kedgeree
Salmon fishcakes
Stuffed pepper boats

Pasta (cooked)
Sausage pasta bake

Peas (frozen)
Frittata
Kedgeree
Pea & ham quiche
Vegetable korma
Vegetable samosas

Pepper
Frittata
Sardine & vegetable
   couscous
Sausage pasta bake
Stuffed pepper boats
Vegetable tart art

Pittas
Pitta chips
Ham & mushroom pizza
Tuna mayo pitta pockets

Plums
Fruit fool

Potato
Frittata
Stuffed pepper potato boats
Vegetable korma
Vegetable samosas

Puff pastry
Cheese straws
Chicken & ham pie
Vegetable tart art

Raspberries
Custard tart
Frozen yoghurt lollies

Raspberry cheesecake

Rice (cooked)
Kedgeree
Egg-free arancini

Salmon (tinned or fresh)
Salmon fishcakes
Salmon & tomato cannelloni

Sausages (cooked)
Sausage pasta bake

Shortcrust pastry
Pea & ham quiche

Shortcrust pastry (sweet)
Custard tart

Spinach (fresh)
Baked fish parcels

Spinach (frozen)
Salmon & tomato cannelloni
Vegetable tart art

Spring onion
Nachos
Salmon fishcakes
Tomato salsa bruschetta

Strawberries
Croissant pudding
Fruit salad rainbow cone
Fruity mess

Sweetcorn
Pirate treasure salad
Sardine & vegetable
   couscous
Tuna mayo pitta pockets

Tomato sauce
Ham & mushroom pizza
Salmon & tomato cannelloni
Sausage pasta bake
Vegetable tart art

Tomatoes
Baked fish parcels
Frittata
Guacamole
Nachos
Pirate treasure salad
Tomato salsa bruschetta

Tarragon
Chicken bread baskets

Tortilla wraps
Curried chicken wraps
Ham & mushroom pizza
Nachos

Vegetables
Baked fish parcels
Salmon & tomato cannelloni
Egg-free arancini
Frittata
Sausage pasta bake
Pea & ham quiche
Sardine & vegetable
   couscous

Vegetable korma
Vegetable samosas
Vegetable tart art

Yoghurt (flavoured)
Frozen yoghurt lollies
Raspberry cheesecake

**Yoghurt (Greek-style/
   natural)**
Bacon & egg soda bread
Carrot cakes
Curried chicken wraps
Blueberry yoghurt muffins
Egg-free cookies
Frozen yoghurt lollies
Fruit fool
Fruity mess
Fruity yoghurt pots
Lemon yoghurt cake
Naan bread
Overnight oats
Tzatziki

Index

Further resources

I keep a constantly evolving list of useful products, blogs, classes and recipe links on www.cookwithtoddlers.com. Also join our Cook With Toddlers Community on Facebook or @cookwithtots on Twitter for regular updates and to share tales, tips and recipes for cooking with toddlers.

Acknowledgements

Thank you . . .
To my agent Heather Holden-Brown and Sam Jackson at Ebury Publishing for your faith in me and this project.

To Katy Denny, Morwenna Loughman and everyone at Ebury.

To the editor Jo Godfrey Wood and designer Peggy Sadler at Bookworx for always seeing what was needed.

To my talented friend Hannah Bennett for writing a poem that captures everything this book is about.

To three inspirational teachers/childcare professionals: Angela Bastable, Emily Foan and Sue Pankow for their early-years' learning wisdom.

To the brilliant team of grown-ups and their little chefs who tested recipes: Claire Allen, Hannah Bennett, Leandra Bramham, Bex Carter, Kate Cole, Jackie Cruse, Lucy Dickson, Kat Gilbert, Emma Hawkins, Hannah Hill, Sarah Holgate, Rachel McConnell, Julie Morgan Webber, Kate Morris, Nathalie Paterson, Sarah Paterson, Rosalind Phillips, Lydia Pyrioxou, Sally Sharpe, Marie-Clare Simpson, Charlie Slight, Jo Spry, Emily Whitechurch, Becky Wilkinson, Karen Wood and Anne Woolmer.

To all those who cook with their children and have encouraged me further, particularly those mentioned above, plus Katie Cone, Sophie Davies, Katy Flint, Sarah Holgate, Rachel Robinson, Jo Sharp, Keely Silver, Lucy Young and those at Little Learning Seeds, Handy Herbs and the Tesco Eat Happy Project.

To all the unbelievably co-operative toddlers who had their photographs taken for this book and to Kitchen Craft and Vibrant Home, who provided some of the equipment featured for a fundraising event.

To my parents for bringing me up to believe in seizing opportunities.

To the rest of my family and close friends for their support and encouragement, especially Patricia Paterson, who made this book happen.

To my own little chefs for their enthusiasm and being my inspiration.

And finally to John for being my harshest critic and greatest champion – I could, and would, never have done any of this without you.